The
Pueblo Revolt
Massacre

Rubén Sálaz Márquez

Dedication

*To Vidal Santillanes and the memory of Millie Santillanes,
sterling Americans who would not be intimidated into being ashamed
of their Spanish New Mexican culture.*

Design and production by David Wilson
Cover art by Orae Dominguez.
Cover photography by Rosemary Sálaz

Limited First Edition

Sálaz Márquez, Rubén
The Pueblo Revolt Massacre
Includes:
1. Anasazi history. 2. New Mexican Pueblo history. 3. Spanish entry and settlement in New Mexico. 4. Oñate colonists. 5. Acoma War. 6. European witchcraft. 7. Pueblo Indian witchcraft. 8. Christian missionaries versus Indian medicine men. 9. Spanish colonial history of New Mexico. 10. Pueblo Revolt. 11. Casualties of the Revolt uprising. 12. Diego de Vargas and his colonists. 13. Alliance of Hispanos and Pueblos. 14. Anza and the Comanche Peace. 15. Review of the literature on the Pueblo Revolt. 16. Analysis of the Literature. 17. Final Analysis and Conclusions.

Manufactured in the United States of America.

ISBN 978-0-932492-08-1

Cosmic House
P.O. Box 7748
Albuquerque, New Mexico 87194
www.historynothype.com

WORKS by RUBEN SALAZ M.

Tabloid
Tierra Amarilla Shootout

History
Cosmic: The La Raza Sketchbook
New Mexico: A Brief Multi-History
EPIC of the Greater Southwest

Educational Materials
Cosmic Posters (bilingual)
Indian Saga Posters

Children's Books
The Cosmic Reader of the Southwest – For Young People

In Spanish
La Lectura Cósmica del Suroeste – Para Los Jóvenes

Short Stories
Heartland: Stories of the Southwest

Novels (trilogy)
I am Tecumseh! (Books I and II)

Dramas
Embassy Hostage: The Drama of Americans in Iran
Tonight or Never!
Dialog of the Dead

Essays
USA Today (Guest Editorials)

Anthologies
Included in: *The Language of Literature* (McDougal Littell); *Cuento
Chicano del siglo XX* (Universidad Nacional Autónoma de México,
Ediciones Coyoacán, New México State University); *Voces: An
Anthology of Nuevo Mexicano Writers* (El Norte Publications);
Tierra: Contemporary Short Fiction of N.M. (Cinco Puntos Press);
Mexican American Short Stories (Reclam, English-German)

TABLE OF CONTENTS

Introduction

~

Noted historian Marc Simmons has observed that history is everywhere apparent in New Mexico. It is true that people have been in the area since at least 12,000 B.C., Europeans and the written word since 1540. How much can we really understand if something happened thousands or even hundreds of years ago? Is an archaeological dig a good source or just an indication for knowledge of the past? How much personal interpretation is involved in archaeology? In studying the written word? The human factor certainly can't be denied when studying History.

Human motivation is complex therefore relating human behavior is no simple feat because every historian holds varying degrees of bias. Further, entire societies can hold beliefs that could be described as biases. How should societal cultural bias be recognized and approached in studying New Mexican history?

There is no denying that bias, pro and con, exists in all cultures. Philip Wayne Powell wrote a book titled *Tree of Hate: Propaganda and Prejudices Affecting United States Relations with the Hispanic World.* Dr. Powell writes that there is a readily discernible American animosity directed toward Spain, its people, and its Church. If this is true, and the reader must decide the matter, then cultural bias must certainly be kept in mind when studying New Mexican history.

Historians and other writers can take the same basic facts and come out with perspectives that are in conflict with each other. So what is *History* and what is *His-Story?* Who is actually a *hero?* A *villain?* Is it possible for one person to be *both?*

It is crucial to study both sides of any issue. This work will provide information not readily encountered in most publications. The intent is to present a more complete historical account than what has been provided in the past. In so doing, both sides will be documented so that the reader may investigate further if so desired. The reader has the choice of whom or what to believe.

Prologue

IF ONE IS INTERESTED IN GENERAL NEW MEXICAN HISTORY YOU are certain to encounter two items which appear constant no matter what era you are investigating: the Acoma War of 1599 and the Pueblo Revolt of 1680. This might sound a bit far fetched so let's document the assertion. Years ago the New Mexico Department of Tourism issued a brochure titled *El Camino Real*, giving some history on this famous "Royal Road," for centuries the longest in North America. The text reads in part: "*...When the Indians, who had been mistreated by the Spanish colonists, organized the Pueblo Revolt of 1680, the camino enabled Governor Antonio de Otermín and the surviving colonists to flee south to safety.*"

While supposedly informing on the *Camino Real*, anyone, visiting tourists included, would certainly get the message that "Spanish colonists" had mistreated the Pueblo Indians, thus causing the Revolt. One might likely ask if such a statement was intended to attract tourists, or perhaps wonder how pertinent it was considering that the topic is the *Royal Road*. Additionally, would such a statement reflect on contemporary Hispanic New Mexicans, especially in Santa Fe?

Assuredly we don't have to go back several years for Black Legend historiography to show itself. As recently as the 2007 Summer Edition of the *New Mexico Historical Review*, a scholarly publication put out by the University of New Mexico, which tells us in an article titled "History Carved in Stone" that after the Acoma War, Oñate "*...decreed that all males 25 years of age lose their right foot and sentenced them to twenty years of personal servitude.*" Is it possible the author and/or the editors of the NMHR don't know the sentence applied only to twenty-four (24) warriors? And should a scholarly publication concern itself with the question of whether or not it was actually carried out? Further, when does common sense become a factor, especially if one considers that a footless man can render very little help in a farm and ranch society? (See below for details on the Acoma War.)

In this scholarly article the Acoma War is used as a warm-up for information on the Pueblo Revolt. (The Summer Edition also contains an article that describes the "controversy" surrounding the monumental Oñate statue in El Paso, Texas.) Even a casual observer might ask why events of 1599 and 1680 are relevant today. These are some of the questions that will be addressed in this short volume.

The Pueblo Revolt of 1680 still appears to be an especially popular topic and the man reputed to be its leader, *Popé,* now often rendered *Po'pay (Ripe Squash* or *Ripe Pumpkin* or *Ripe Cultigens* in the literature) is in Statuary Hall representing New Mexico along with Senator Dennis Chávez. Unique among Indian uprisings in what is now the USA, the entire event seems to be endowed with superlative goals as time marches on. For example, the Revolt has been described as *"The first American Revolution."*[1]

Is it possible that typical American historiographers have a special concern for the general welfare of Pueblo people and/or Amerindians in general? What factors are at work here?

History in what is now New Mexico and the Southwest is a complexity of at least five layers of information: Precontact Amerindian, Spanish, Mexican, American, and Friendly/Hostile Amerindians. Much Amerindian history has been derived from archaeological and anthropological sources, as well as testimony from native informants during contact with European-based people generally writing in either Spanish or English. The Spanish presence started with Coronado in 1540 (the first settlement was made in 1598) and ended in 1821. History for that period, and certainly that of the Pueblo Revolt, was written in the Spanish language so Spanish documentation has to be utilized, though this has also been criticized in some quarters.

The area was Mexican territory until around 1846 when the USA invaded and took over. New Mexican history began to be written in English with the appearance of Americans in the 19th century. How American history is written becomes an issue in the writing of New Mexican and Southwest history.

Writing accurate History is no simple feat. There are many factors at play. Not only must the writer be acquainted with sources, s/he must present them faithfully in order to be valid. It is simple to relate what one wishes to be the case, especially if the reading public is unfamiliar with the issue at hand. Further, many writers descend into "analysis," which often projects historiography into the realm of essays though the reader is often unaware s/he is reading the author's opinion.

Another major pitfall in American historiography is *presentism:* judging events of centuries ago by contemporary standards. For example, in the 1600s whipping a guilty person was an acceptable punishment throughout Europe when decided upon in a court of law whereas today it would be considered "cruel and unusual punishment." It must be kept in mind that accepted customs of centuries ago are being dealt with when studying New Mexican or Southwest history during the era of New Spain.

Also a major pitfall is permitting *cultural bias* to color one's writing. In this type of propaganda under the guise of History, the "good guys" are always your own and the "bad guys" are always on the other side, no matter what the facts are.

Have American historiographers been able to utilize Spanish language documentation when writing about the Pueblo Revolt? How has such documentation been approached? One must always investigate the sources consulted for the Revolt and how faithful has been the translation of Spanish language documents by writers of History. Why? Because we find glaring errors in translation even for relatively simple phrases like *llano estacado,* which is generally translated into English as "staked plains." In reality it means *palisaded* or *stockaded plains,* which is what tablelands looked like from afar. [2] If a simple phrase like *llano estacado* can be mistranslated and the mistranslation is widely accepted, what might be happening to Spanish language documents describing more complex issues?

One should also ask: Is Amerindian oral history more reliable than Spanish language documentation? What is the validity of Pueblo oral history? Is it like folklore? Can it be investigated? Is oral tradition comparable to recorded documents?

SPECIAL STATUS of the PUEBLOS

When writing about the Pueblo people of New Mexico one must also keep in mind an additional factor: they enjoy a very special place in New Mexican society. There are many books that can be cited to document this observation, which will be done below, but for the time being as an example one need only go buy some gasoline on Indian reservations. The price per gallon is about the same on or off the reservation yet Indians are exempt from paying State gasoline taxes. In a word, the tax is charged to the customer but not paid to the State, the Pueblos being exempt from such taxes.

On the academic level, many Hispano and non-Hispano writers alike promote this special status. In a nutshell, it is not customary to bring out anything about the Pueblos that could be construed as derogatory. An example of this out of history is the fact that the Pueblos were described as living in polygamous societies by some of the first Euro observers in New Mexico. The truth be told, most Amerindians lived polygamous life styles and this included Pueblos as well as Apaches, and Navajos.

Pueblo polygamy comes as a surprise to most readers. This despite the fact that Gaspar de Villagrá, author of New Mexico's founding chronicle,

Historia de la Nueva Mexico, 1610, explicitly states in Canto XV:

> *We visited a good many of these pueblos...The men have as many wives as they can support...* [3]

Noted scholar Dr. Gilberto Espinosa did the translation for the above quoted work that was published in 1933 by the Río Grande Press out of Chicago. Then on page 146, Note # 21, Espinosa writes: *"This statement is incorrect for the Pueblo Indians have always been noted as monogamists..."* So here we have quite a spectacle: Villagrá describes the Pueblo people as polygamists while Dr. Espinosa, a 20th century writer, says Villagrá, an eye witness at the time, 1598 and after, *"is incorrect..."* So who is the reader to believe if not eyewitness Villagrá? Why does Dr. Espinosa contradict his Villagrá documentation?

Let us investigate other editions. Dr. Ramón Gutiérrez, author of *When Jesús Came, the Corn Mothers Went Away,* using a 1933 Villagrá text published in Los Ángeles, writes that Pueblo *"...heads of successful households were often polygamous...The men have as many wives as they can support..."* He also quotes one (Captain) Marcelo de Espinosa as saying: *"I saw Indians who had five or six wives..."* Other observers also recorded that *"...the number of wives one had depended on rank, for it is a mark of prestige to have numerous wives."* [4]

In the *Fray Alonso de Benavides Revised Memorial of 1634* edited by George P. Hammond, Fr. Benavides writes that Christian progress was being made but of the Taos Nation he said: *"In this pueblo they had a custom which the others had not, that is, a man had as many wives as he could support...it was still difficult to extirpate this evil from among them."* [5]

The dispassionate observer will conclude that polygamy was an integral part of Pueblo society and lifestyle. It was part of their pre-Christian traditions. So why do some writers shy away from that fact? Some might assert they don't so let's provide one more example. The University of New Mexico Press issued the classic Villagrá work in a bilingual edition in 1992. Part of the very excellent *Pasó Por Aqui* series, the book was billed as *"A Critical and Annotated Spanish/English Edition Translated and Edited by Miguel Encinias, Alfred Rodriguez, and Joseph P. Sánchez."* In Canto XV of this *Historia de la Nueva Mexico, 1610* work can be found the information (p. 142):

> *...That the maidens, when once they mature,*
> *They are common to all without excuse,*
> *Provided that they pay...*

So unmarried Pueblo males could have condoned sexual union with single

Pueblo maidens provided they could pay for it. Yet when it comes to Pueblo polygamy, the authors see fit to relegate it to footnote #3 in this fashion:

> "...*see Villagrá, Historia, Junquera edition, 229. See also p. 234 for Villagrá's reference to POLYGAMY.*" [*Emphasis added.*]

The original work is that of Villagrá so why did the translators decide to omit that part of the original and instead direct the reader to the archives? Why would these well-known scholars and a scholarly press skirt the issue of Pueblo polygamy? Perhaps because of the special place Pueblo people have in New Mexican society? Has that attitude among writers had something to do with Pueblo history, specifically with the volumes written on the Pueblo Revolt? We shall see.

Sources

The basic source for this present work is the classic *Revolt of the Pueblo Indians of New Mexico and Otermín's Attempted Reconquest, 1680-1682* by Charles Wilson Hackett with the translation of Spanish language documents by Dr. Charmion Clair Shelby. Quotations from this scholarly, two-volume work are so numerous that only the first will be cited individually. Additional sources will be cited and footnoted with the general reading public in mind. The intent here is to provide a readable but historically accurate book for the reader of history.

Documentation for PROLOGUE

1. The issue of Amerindian history is complex. Indian wars in what is now the continental United States started with the Powhatan wars of 1609-13, 1622-32, and 1644-46. Before 1680 there was also King Philip's War in 1675. All of these took place before the Pueblo Revolt of 1680.

The American "Westward Movement" is replete with Indian wars. It can also be observed that American Indian wars didn't end until the slaughter of Big Foot and some 250 people of his Sioux band at Wounded Knee in 1890. Are these tragedies as popular as the Acoma War and the Pueblo Revolt?

2. It is indeed absurd to believe that Spaniards used wooden stakes with which to find their way on the trackless Great Plains. For example, from how far away can you see a wooden stake driven into the ground? And where would they have obtained the wood to make the stakes in the first place? The Great Plains have no forests and Spaniards explored all the way from New Mexico and Texas to Kansas. Despite these obvious facts, most writers still mention *"the Staked Plains."*

3. Espinosa, Gilberto. *A History of New Mexico*. Chicago: Río Grande

Press, 1933, p. 143.

4. Gutiérrez, Ramón. *When Jesús Came, the Corn Mothers Went Away.* Stanford: Stanford University Press, 1991, p. 12.

5. Hammond, George P. (ed.) *Fray Alonso de Benavides Revised Memorial of 1634.* Albuquerque: University of New Mexico Press, 1945, p. xxxvi.

Part I
Amerindian Background

~

S PEAKING GENERALLY, THERE WERE HUMAN BEINGS IN NEW Mexico and the Southwest by around 12,000 B.C. (though some say people arrived much earlier). The group known as *Anasazi,* said to be the ancestors of Pueblo people, were Stone Age beings at first dressed in animal skins and users of stone tools. They used fire pits built inside rooms and had domesticated dogs. The bow and arrow was unknown to them until later but they used the atlatl to hunt large game animals. From a stone age level, the Anasazi group is credited with eventually creating a highly developed culture, for the time and place, and building wonders like Pueblo Bonito "Great Houses."

Agriculture consisted of raising basic crops like corn, beans, and squash. Climactic changes forced the people to move often, abandoning established villages and building new ones. Drought was a constant menace for a people who often had to live mostly by gathering with hunting whenever possible.

Despite the grandeur of the later "Great Houses," Anasazi life was difficult and survival no simple feat. Health conditions were poor. Large numbers of children perished. Even at the relatively affluent Chaco Canyon area, children under five years of age comprised some 26% of all burials. In other areas it was some 45%. It has been estimated that only around 50% of young people made it to the age of 18.

Ordinary people suffered from malnutrition, anemia, parasites from constant animal contact, diarrhea, overcrowded conditions, and unpurified water. Women suffered from anemia and arthritic conditions of the spine from too much stoop labor and carrying heavy loads. Men and women suffered from severe dental cavities, tooth erosion, and serious periodontal disease. On average, men lived some seven years longer than women. The elites of Chaco Canyon, who probably had better food, averaged around two inches taller than those who did the work.

Prehistoric warfare will be addressed below but it is important to make certain observations at this time. According to archaeologists, evidence of warfare in Anasazi society was constant until about A.D. 900 to around 1150. Perhaps due to a beneficent climate, which permitted the raising of sufficient food, there was no need to compete for agricultural territory or basic food supplies. Resources were not stressed and populations increased until they caught up with the land's carrying capacity. Without the threat of war, there were cultural interactions between groups as well as a lively trade.

Things changed. From around 1150 on, death by violent means appears once again to have become a constant threat in Anasazi society. Archaeologists have uncovered mass graves of people who died violently after around 1150. They have concluded that various groups fought to the death in vicious hand-to-hand battles. Sites have been excavated that revealed dismembered and decapitated bodies of men, women, and children. It has been estimated that some 60% of adults and perhaps 38% of children died violently. [1]

C.G. Turner and J.A. Turner described a most controversial view of Anasazi society during this time. They stated that cannibalism appeared among the Anasazi, an *"interpretation of violence and cannibalism so contrary to prevailing concepts of the peaceful Pueblo Indians."* Of the 76 sites investigated by Turner, 38 sites showed evidence of cannibalism due to the way flesh was scraped off human bones, as well as other indications. *"Evidence is concentrated in the Anasazi culture area...It is within the Chacoan sphere of influence that cannibalized human remains occur most often."* [2] The evidence consists of bones broken and burned, cut and scrape marks on the bones, bones broken to get at the marrow, bones cut to fit storage or cooking containers. Bodies of humans were processed the same as if they were the carcasses of animals

Turner postulates that perhaps it was *"...the arrival of a Mexican force,"* accustomed to cannibalism as ritual, intimidation, and social control, which introduced the practice in the Southwest. Turner writes that *"...dental transfigurement (as found on Mexican Indians) suggest cannibalism might be a Mexican import..."* and that *"After the abandonment of Chaco, human sacrifice and cannibalism all but disappeared."* [3]

The drought that started in 1130 was definitely the eventual death knell for Anasazi society in general. Anasazi achievements were over by about A.D. 1200 when, it is written, the various groups moved to areas along the Río Grande River where they became the Pueblo people.

WARFARE in PREHISTORIC TIMES

Despite the impression that Pueblo people were basically peaceful agriculturalists, it would appear that populations in the Southwest were as addicted to war as were Europeans. It must be remembered that while aborigines are referred to as *Indians,* implying they are one group, the diverse Pueblo people were Piro, Keresan, Hopi, Zuni, and Tano (which included the subgroups of Towa, Tewa, and Tiwa), as different from each other as the varying ethnic groups in Europe who have always made war on each other.

From the time of the Anasazi to villages found by the Spanish, who named them *pueblos,* it appears warfare was a fact of life in the Southwest.[1] Raiding parties, hit-and-run attacks, scalping, pillaging, ambushes, massacres, etc., and taking captives were common activities before European contact. Steven LeBlanc and other writers assert that entire societies were exterminated because they could not defend themselves against their enemies. Indeed, the very fact of *village dwelling populations* was created as a defense to savage warfare in the Precontact Southwest. Perhaps the best examples of obvious defensive sites are the *Sky City* of Acoma high atop a mesa in New Mexico and the "cliff dwellings" of Mesa Verde in Colorado.

LeBlanc asserts that warfare among Amerindians has little to do with Europeans entering the Southwest. Archaeological digs have uncovered irrefutable evidence in the number of prehistoric villages established on sites good for defense, of unburied burned bodies, numbers of burned villages, bodies that show evidence of violent death, and mass graves which contained not only men but women and children. So-called "primitive" warfare was indeed deadly for males and significantly high for women and children (higher than the death rates for Europe in the 20th century, according to LeBlanc).

What caused Amerindian wars and massacres? Perhaps people fought over limited resources necessary for survival. Perhaps they fought for revenge, perhaps to obtain women, perhaps to acquire status. Strategies included the ambush, the surprise attack, the siege of hundreds of warriors intending to overrun a settlement, the massacre of the entire enemy. If all this is accurate, genocide was the purpose of Precontact warfare.

Prehistoric weaponry evolved from atlatls, bow (from a stave of wood) and arrows, slings, spears, shields, and wooden swords. The "sinew-backed recurved bow" (a reinforced bow; thought to have been introduced from Asia) was a gigantic step forward because of its penetrating qualities. Arrows shot from a recurved bow could go right through previous shields so now shields had to be reinforced with buffalo hide. If all warriors owned a shield, this would indicate a lively trade with Indians from the Great Plains.

For hand-to-hand fighting the favorite weapon was probably the club, usually made of wood or deer antlers. Daggers were made of bone or horn.

By around A.D. 1300 there were few small villages along the Río Grande Valley because most sites were now large, probably because a large population

9

could mount a good defense against attackers. As already mentioned, sites were selected and villages built with defense in mind because the Southwest was now engulfed in constant warfare. (This situation is documented by archaeological sites which have revealed burned villages, burned bodies, unburied bodies, etc., and from Precontact art on walls and pottery.)

Prevailing military strategy after 1300 appears to have been total extermination of a community then burning the entire village to the ground. Crops were targeted because by laying waste to cornfields the enemy could be defeated through starvation, which would target the entire society, combatants and non-combatants.

If you didn't live in a fortress community, chances of survival were slim. Migration to large villages was therefore necessary for self-preservation. In a large village stronghold the people could store necessary supplies of food, water, and weaponry. Hundreds of defenders would be readily available for defense. If another village had to be attacked, there would be plenty of warriors remaining behind to defend against a counterattack.

No Río Grande Valley group appears to have been dominant over the others so it has been said that most Pueblo groups survived. There was no central government. All were independent of everybody else. Relationships between pueblos appear to have changed constantly from alliance to counteralliance. There developed large, unpopulated buffer zones between Pueblo fortress villages.

So who was *the enemy?* Did the Pueblos fight each other? As already mentioned, they were totally different groups of people. Or was it the appearance of Athapaskan people, Apache and Navajo, which started the warfare of annihilation? Those questions have not been answered.

The reader should be aware that the foregoing is based on archaeological findings. Can these findings be accepted as *History?* If an archaeological site indicates, for example, that the recurved bow came from Asia and pottery came from Mexico, should those assertions be a part of the historical record? The reader must decide what to believe.

Documentation for AMERINDIAN BACKGROUND

1. Stuart, David. *Anasazi America.* Albuquerque: University of New Mexico Press, 2000, p. 128.

2. Turner, C.G., Turner, J.A. *MAN CORN: Cannibalism and Violence in the Prehistoric Southwest.* Salt Lake City: University of Utah Press, 1999, pp. 6, 55, 459. Christy Turner is much maligned and quite correct when he states his discovery is alien to anyone who has written about the Anasazi. To my knowledge, no one else has popularized cannibalism as part of Anasazi society. For example, David Stuart's work on the Anasazi published a year

after Turner's, doesn't mention cannibalism at all. Is it possible a scholar like Dr. Stuart was unaware of Turner's controversial book?

3. *MAN CORN,* pp. 470, 483-4.

4. LeBlanc, Steven A. *Prehistoric Warfare in the American Southwest.* Salt Lake City: University of Utah Press, 1999, pp. 4, 9, 23, passim. LeBlanc writes (p. 41): *"...archaeologists have regularly ignored evidence for prehistoric warfare, in spite of evidence that shows it was very common."* Like Christy Turner, Steven Leblanc might be criticized for his work on prehistoric warfare because it doesn't follow the usual pattern.

11

Part II
Euro Entrada & Settlement
~

FRANCISCO VÁSQUEZ DE CORONADO LED THE FIRST EURO exploration into New Mexico and the Southwest in 1540. For the first time there would be a European culture in the area, a culture which included Christianity, the wheel and wheeled vehicles, horses, cattle, wheat, etc., Euro mining technology, etc., and a written language with which to record events, among many other aspects of Spanish European civilization.

Pedro de Castaneda was the soldier-chronicler for the expedition and H.E. Bolton's classic work states *"...Alvarado gives us our first view of the Río Grande Valley above Albuquerque..."* The Tigua Indians of the Bernalillo area are described as *"good people, devoted more to agriculture than to war..."* though he was to learn later how well they could fight. They lived basically on maize, beans, melons and lots of turkeys. They dressed in cotton clothes, also skins of cattle [buffalo], with coats made of turkey feathers. *"They wear their hair short..."* and *"...the old men are the ones who have most authority among them."* Alvarado's group went up to the populous Taos Pueblo where the natives were friendly. When Alvarado went east he visited Pecos Pueblo (Cicúique) and saw firsthand the Pueblo peoples' *"...lively trade in slaves maintained by the Plains tribes with the Pueblos of the upper Rio Grande from earliest times to the nineteenth century."*[1] It is obvious that human slavery was as much a part of Precontact Pueblo society as it was common in European countries of that time.

FOUNDING of HISPANIC NEW MEXICO
Juan de Oñate was awarded the contract to colonize, at his own expense, the land of New Mexico, which settlement would be some 800 miles north of the closest Christian settlement in New Spain. Bureaucratic delays, during which Oñate had to pay all expenses, almost destroyed the expedition but the 500 or so Christians were finally permitted to travel north. They

celebrated their thanksgiving entry into New Mexico on April 30, 1598 in the area of present El Paso/Juarez. (This is the first Thanksgiving to be celebrated in what is now the USA, if one doesn't count the celebration held by Coronado.)

OÑATE Colonists

Who were these first pioneers of a European-American culture in what is now the Southwest? They were the following colonists who accompanied Governor Juan de Oñate to *San Juan de los Caballeros* (Knights of St. John; shortly they moved to San Gabriel and then around 1607-1608 to Santa Fe, New Mexico) many of them with families:

A:
Pablo de Aguilar;
Araujo;
Ascencio de Archuleta;
Ayarde;

B:
Dionisio de Bañuelos;
Bartol;
Juan Benitez;
Bibero;
Juan Gutiérrez de Bocanegra;
Juan Pérez de Bustillo (with his wife, María de la Cruz, a son, and three
    daughters);

C:
Cesar Ortíz Cadimo;
Juan Camacho;
Esteban Carabajal;
Carrera;
Juan de Caso;
Bernabé de las Casas;
Castillo;
Juan Catalán;
Cavanillas;
Gregorio César;
Cordero;
Juan Cortés; Marcos Cortés;

13

D:
Pedro Sánchez Damiero;
Juan Díaz;
Juan Pérez de Donis;

E:
Felipe Escalte;
Juan Escarramal;
Marcelo de Espinosa;

F:
Marcos Farfán de los Godos;
Juan Fernández;
Manuel Francisco;

G:
Alvaro García; Francisco García; Francisco García; Marcos García; Simón
  García;
Luis Gascón;
Bartolomé González; Juan González;
Juan Griego;
Guevara;
Francisco Guillén;
Antonio Gutiérrez;

H:
Gerónimo de Heredia;
Antonio Hernández; Francisco Hernández; Gonzalo Hernández; Pedro
  Hernández;
Antonio Conde de Herrera; Cristóbal de Herrera; Juan de Herrera;
Alonzo Nuñez de Hinojosa;

I:
León de Isati;

J:
Jiménez;

L:
Diego Landin;
Francisco de Ledesma;

14

Juan de León;
Domingo de Lizana;
Cristóbal López; Juan López;
Alonso Lucas;
Lucio;

M:
Mallea;
Francisco Márquez; Gerónimo Márquez;
Hernán Martín;
Juan Martínez;
Juan Medel;
Medina;
Monroi;
Alonso Gómez Montesinos;
Baltazar de Monzón;
Morales;
Juan Moran;
Munera;

N:
Naranjo;
Diego Nuñez;

O:
Juan de Olague;
Cristóbal de Oñate;
Juan de Ortega;
Ortiz;

P:
Regundo Paladín;
Simón de Paz;
Juan de Pedraza;
Pereya;
Simón Pérez;
Juan Pinero;
Francisco de Posa y Peñalosa;

Q:
Alonso de Quesada;

Francisco Guillén de Quesada;

R:
Martín Ramiréz;
Juan Rangel;
Rascón;
Pedro de los Reyes;
Pedro de Ribera;
Alonso del Río;
Diego Robledo; Francisco Robledo; Pedro Robledo (the first colonist to die in NM) with his wife, Catalina López;
Pedro Rodríguez; Sebastián Rodríguez;
Bartolomé Romeros;
Moreno de la Rua;
Capt. Ruiz; Juan Ruiz;

S:
Lorenzo Salado;
Juan de Salas;
Alonso Sánchez; Cristóbal Sánchez; Francisco Sánchez;
Antonio Sarinana;
Juan de Segura;
Serrano;
Sosa;

T:
Capt. Tabora;

V:
Francisco Vaca;
Varela;
Francisco Vásquez;
Jorge de la Vega;
Juan Velarde;
Francisco Vido;
Juan de Victoria Vido;
Gaspar Pérez de Villagrá;
Villalba;
Villaviciosa;

Z:
Juan de Zaldívar; Vicente de Zaldívar;
León Zapata;
Zubia;
Zumaia

As indicated above, on July 11 Oñate established a Christian settlement named *San Juan de los Caballeros*, the Knights of St. John, in a Tewa Indian village called Okhay Owingeh, in what is now the Española Valley. By August 18 the colonists arrived at their new home but which was shortly moved to another location they called *San Gabriel*. It was some 800 miles away from Santa Barbara, the closest Christian town in New Spain.

The little colony was almost 2000 miles from Mexico City and the trail blazed would become known as the *Camino Real (of the Interior),* for several centuries the longest road in North America. Hispanic settlement was also the beginning of ranching and mining (which were to become integral parts of the much later American West).

There was trouble almost immediately because fully a third of the officers and soldiers were totally disillusioned with their circumstances. They plotted to abandon this *worthless wilderness* and return to civilization in New Spain. (Oñate was later to write that this group was angry over not finding bars of silver on the ground and his refusal to allow them to work the Indians like slaves.)

Oñate sent out messengers calling for Pueblo leaders to meet at *Khe-wa* village (now Santo Domingo). Some 38 Indian leaders attend the meeting and through interpreters Oñate explains his colonizing effort to the Amerindians. They appear to accept the new colony but later a minor chieftain from Acoma, a man named Zutucapán, lets it be known he doesn't want the newcomers to stay. He wants to start a war and destroy the new colony. Zutucapán thought this could be easily done. After all, Acoma village alone had more people than the entire Christian colony. Zutucapán had only to convince his people.

Villagrá took up where Castaneda left off in describing the village *(Pueblo)* people of what has come to be termed New Mexico, which obviously did not have that name before the Euro settlement. [2]

As mentioned above, Canto XV of the Gilberto Espinosa translation of Villagrá's epic states, *"We visited a good many of these pueblos...the men have as many wives as they can support..."* He also observed that the Pueblo people had a "base and vile custom..." specifically that their *"damsels are common property for all while they are single."* Apparently the swain with the most gifts could buy sexual favors. It is also stated that once the Pueblo woman was married she was required to be faithful to her one husband. A custom among the Pueblos was that an adulterous woman could be punished by having her nose and ears cut off. (Adultery could be punished by putting the offenders to death among the later arriving Comanches.)

It can be observed that Pueblo men could have sexual partners before marriage, if they could pay, and they could also have several wives at the same time, if the women could be supported, so sexual access could be described as a major consideration in Pueblo society.

Villagrá also states that the Pueblo people *"...were addicted to the bestial wicked sin."* He tells of a youth in the group who was *"...attacked by a savage..."* but failed in his intent because the young man yelled out for help and the *"savage took to his heels."*

The 1992 UNM Press edition of *Historia* corroborates the above sexual activities of the Pueblos but, curiously, in footnote # 3 on page 142 the reader is informed:

> *"The Curtis manuscript with which we work in the Coronado Room of the UNM Library does not translate these lines. For the tolerance of homosexuality among the ancient Pueblo Indians, see Villagrá, Historia, Junquera edition, 229.*[3]

18

ACOMA

During the month of October, Oñate toured various pueblos by way of getting to know them. Unknown to the Captain General, Zutucapán and a war faction at the mesa-top village of Acoma had decided to assassinate Oñate in order to start a war of extermination against the newcomers.

Oñate and his men were invited to go up to the Sky City and meet the people. Once there, Oñate was invited to go into the kiva to see *a marvelous treasure.* But it was for Oñate alone, not his men. The Adelantado was a frontiersman who had much experience with Indians so he became suspicious immediately and declined the invitation. (A few weeks later he learned that a dozen Indians were waiting for him in the dark kiva, placed there by Zutucapán, waiting to kill him in order to start a war.) Oñate and his men descended from the mesa top and continued their tour of Pueblo land.

In December Oñate's nephew Juan de Zaldívar and his 31 men stop at Acoma for a previously agreed upon trade of hatchets, etc., for flour. With a few soldiers left behind to guard the horses, Zaldívar and 18 men climb to the top and are told the flour is waiting for them at different houses around the village. The Christians are therefore separated as they are led in different directions. Suddenly, by some secret signal, the Spaniards are attacked from all sides throughout the village. From terraces Acoma men and women hurl large stones at them, warriors shoot at them with arrows then charge at them with war clubs. Still not recognizing the premeditated ambush, Juan de Zaldívar orders his men to fire their harquebusiers into the air to scare the Indians. Then he receives an arrow in his leg and realizes he and his men must fight for their very lives. *The Acomas were intent on exterminating them!* Zaldívar, not yet thirty years of age, uses his sword to drive back his attackers but he is quickly surrounded and Zutucapán gives him a deathblow on the forehead. *"Zaldívar fell, delivered unto that eternal sleep to which we are all doomed someday."*[4]

The unequal fight becomes bloody hand-to-hand combat as sheer numbers drive some of the Christians against a rock wall until the Spaniards fall to the ground where their heads are split open by war clubs and large stones. The Acomas strip the dead Spaniards of their helmets, coats of mail, swords, etc., then hurl the bodies over the cliff, jeering at the small group far below.

A small group of Hispanos fight their way to the edge of the mesa top as the Acomas close in on them. Death being certain if they stay, the Christians jump over the side and miraculously, 3 survive by landing in the wind blown sand dunes far below.

Captain Gerónimo Márquez, an able frontiersman with much experience in Indian warfare, takes charge of the remnant band of Christians. He realizes full well how an Indian uprising can spread throughout the entire province so he decides their first duty is to ride for home at *San Juan* to let the colonists know they must prepare for the worst. The handful of Christian survivors flees the scene before the Indians come down to exterminate them. Later the Acomas come upon the horses that stray from the riders and the animals are slaughtered by filling them full of arrows.

New Mexico's first Christmas in 1598 is one of gloom and sadness. Everyone realizes that the little Christian colony is teetering on the brink of extermination. If other Indian villages unite with the Acomas, extermination of the little colony would be a certainty.

Christmas Mass is the only ray of optimism in the Christian settlement facing extinction so it becomes a ray of hope illuminating the path of survival. Its pageantry in the San Juan Bautista church gives the new colonists some hope. Surely the Almighty would favor their efforts in this great wilderness.

In January 1599, the Captain General convenes a tribunal to discuss what should be done. Oñate knew and understood the King's Law that war with Indians should be avoided if at all possible. Various men state that Acoma must be conquered or there will never be any security in New Mexico. A survivor of the Acoma ambush testifies that the Acomas had acted with premeditation, that they knew full well the attack was coming because they had weapons at the ready. Others stated that if the

Acomas gained the upper hand, Spaniards knowing their mode of warfare, Christian wives and children would not be spared by the savages. The Franciscan missionaries observed that a just war could be declared against the Acomas because the killing of Spaniards was unprovoked. However, the Acomas must first be given an opportunity to make peace and only if they refused could war be declared.

The decision being unanimous, Oñate declares a war of blood and fire against Acoma. No quarter would be asked or given and the Captain General himself would lead it. But then the clergy and colonists convince him that he should not lead the risky campaign because if the Christians should be defeated the Governor would have to lead them out of New Mexico. So Oñate appoints his other nephew, twenty-five-year-old Vicente de Zaldívar, to lead the expedition. Vicente is given 72 men with which to conquer what had been described as the best-situated stronghold in all of North America.

Despite the very real crisis, Oñate instructs his nephew: *"Make more use of clemency than severity if it should turn out that the Acomas have committed their crimes more from incapacity of reason than from malice."*

The heavily armed column leaves the Knights of St. John settlement on January 12, 1599. Only a small number of soldiers remain behind with the worried colonists who have heard that the other Indian villages are preparing an attack on the colony. But doña Eufemia, wife of Francisco de Sosa Peñalosa, leads a contingent of women who inform Oñate they are ready to fight in defense of their settlement. Henceforth the women, dressed like soldiers, appear on the rooftops, ready for whatever move the Indians might make. They stand watch in the bitter cold, marching up and down in military step, ready to fight if the Indians attack.

Vicente de Zaldívar and his men arrive at Acoma within nine days. Working with a translator who speaks the Acoma language, three times Zaldívar informs the jeering Indians they must surrender or they will be attacked. They answer with war whoops, insults, and challenges: *"...crowds of men and women were seen upon the walls dancing stark naked in an orgy of defiance and insult."*[5] They ridicule the puny army down below, saying it will be slaughtered then afterward the Acomas will destroy the Indian villages that helped the Spaniards by giving them food. Like a knight out of the Middle Ages, Zaldívar warns the Acomas to prepare for battle because the Spaniards will wage a war of no quarter.

The little Christian army realized it was taking on a very difficult challenge. The village atop a high mesa was all but unassailable. But young Zaldívar exhorted his men to fight like Spaniards and the victory would be complete. He reminded them that if the Christians didn't win then the entire colony would be slaughtered, which was more than mere rhetoric.

He devised a plan that would feign a frontal attack while a dozen Spaniards would climb to the top from the back. The plan was simple but daring and cunning enough to work.

The attack up the main stepway was started with blaring trumpets and the Indians gathered there to repulse it. The warriors apparently didn't notice the dozen soldiers who went to the far side of the giant rock and climbed to the top without resistance. The ruse had worked! The Indians then saw the Spaniards and attacked with some 400 warriors. It was close quarter, hand to hand fighting. There were times when sheer numbers appeared to win the bloody victory for the Acomas but the Hispanics fought like tigers in return. Zaldívar saw an Indian wearing his dead brother's clothes so he fought his way to him and with a mighty swing of his sword cleaved his skull apart.

The bloody battle didn't abate until nightfall. The Christian beachhead held through the night and more soldiers came up by morning. The two culverin cannon were hauled up by ropes and when they boomed out their death and destruction the air was filled with the stench of burned gunpowder. The tide of battle had turned as the Spaniards set fire to the houses, where some defenders chose to die instead of surrendering.

Hundreds of Acomas killed each other to avoid capture while some threw themselves down the cliff rather than surrender. By the end of the third day the Acomas knew they had lost the war so they surrendered. Some 500 survivors, mostly women and children, were taken captive.

The Acomas were put on trial on February 9, 1599, with Captain Alonso Gómez Montesinos assigned to defend the accused. His basic strategy is a call for clemency because the Indians were behaving according to their own customs and didn't reason like Europeans. The trial ends in three days, with the following results:

No Acoma is given a death sentence.

The Captain General issues guilty sentences for 24 warriors who will have pies, feet (or was it *puntas de pies,* toes?) cut off. (See Pros and Cons below.)

They and all males aged 12 to 25 must render twenty years of servitude.

Women over 12 years of age must render twenty years of servitude.

Children under 12 are free of all guilt and will be under the charge of the priests and nephew Zaldívar who will insure a Christian upbringing; etc.

Two Moquis fighting with the Acomas are to have their right hands cut off then set free.

Marc Simmons sums up: *"The Acomas, however, proved more resilient and slippery...for within a year or two most of them escaped their servitude, returned to their rock, and rebuilt a new pueblo that remains occupied to this day."*

Analysis: DISMEMBERMENT PROS and CONS

Despite the passing of more than four centuries, Juan de Oñate and the Acoma War are still being written about by historians and other writers in and out of New Mexico. What is at the root of this phenomenon? This issue must be addressed before we continue for it has a bearing on how History is written in New Mexico and the American Southwest.

First it must be pointed out, seldom done by most writers, that no Acoma received a death sentence for killing members of the Spanish party that went up to trade, no Acoma was executed for starting the war, or for taking part in it. It must be remembered this was in 1599. In a much later era, which should probably be considered more enlightened or humane, after the Sioux uprising of 1862 in Minnesota, some 400 Sioux were sentenced to death by hanging. President Lincoln, who finally decided that only thirty-eight (38) Sioux would be put to death, set this vicious sentence aside. These actions were more than two and a half centuries apart yet Oñate didn't execute any Acomas in 1599. It can also be said that at an even later date, the end of World War II, German leaders were sentenced to death by Americans at Nuremberg, a fate that also befell some of the Japanese military after Japan surrendered.

Was a dismemberment sentence evidence of *Spanish cruelty* as is so often charged? To understand the history of centuries ago the reader must not fall into the trap of *presentism* (judging events of the past by contemporary standards or behaviors). While considered "cruel and unusual punishment" today, whippings and dismemberments were accepted punishments in all European courts at that time. Dismemberments were not a deviation from ordinary European practice since they were part of the legal system in New Mexico.

Since Spanish language documentation is often questioned as to veracity, one can ask if the sentence of dismemberments against 24 Acoma warriors is accurate history. As mentioned above, the epic poem written by Gaspar Pérez de Villagrá is Hispanic New Mexico's founding chronicle. Cantos 28 to 34 deal specifically with the Acoma War but do not address the sentencing or the dismemberments. It can be said with historical accuracy that Villagrá is not the source for the dismemberment story.

H.H. Bancroft's work titled *History of Arizona and New Mexico, 1530-1888*, states that while Acoma fighters were slaughtered, hundreds of

Acomas killed each other to avoid capture while others threw themselves down the cliff rather than surrender. Bancroft does not mention anything about cutting off feet or hands. Bancroft is not the source for the dismemberment story.

It would appear the dismemberment punishments came from George Hammond and Agapito Rey in their two volume work *Don Juan de Oñate: Colonizer of New Mexico, 1595-1628,* published by UNM Press in 1953. Hammond and Rey assert that twenty-four men were sentenced to have *pies,* feet, cut off, and that the sentence was carried out in various pueblos.

In a personal interview, author/researcher Dr. Eloy Gallegos stated he had seen the document that specified *puntas de pies,* toes, were ordered to be cut off. Is it possible Hammond and Rey mistranslated *puntas de pies,* toes, as *pies,* feet? To be absolutely certain, the original document would have to be located and scrutinized.

Dr. John Kessell, founder of the Vargas Project at the University of New Mexico, has stated his professional researchers/paleographers never found the document that *verified* the dismemberment sentence had actually been carried out. Spaniards have been described as the best of record keepers so one would expect the final act to be recorded (in triplicate, as was the custom). Is it possible the order was given but never carried out?

What is the reader to believe? Hammond and Rey say 24 men had a foot cut off, Eloy Gallegos declares the order was to cut off toes, and John Kessell says there is no documentation verifying the order was ever carried out.

It must also be pointed out that the warriors were sentenced to twenty years of servitude and one can rightly ask what kind of service could a man render if he had to hop around on one foot? Further, not a single missionary or any other observer ever wrote down that he had seen a footless Indian in New Mexico, not even the missionaries who returned to Acoma to minister after the disastrous war. Finally, as already noted by Marc Simmons, the Acomas escaped their servitude after a couple of years and returned to rebuild their Sky City, which is there to this day. Therefore it can be said with certainty that at least part of the sentence was not carried out and the authorities apparently acquiesced to that fact.

Oñate was not out for revenge. Marc Simmons reminds us that even after the Acomas had killed his soldiers, including his nephew, by ambush, he instructed his surviving nephew: *"Make more use of clemency than severity if it should turn out that the Acomas have committed their crimes more from incapacity of reason than from malice."*

It is obvious Oñate was not an Indian hating frontiersmen. Simmons has also written that Oñate's aim was to have the Indians look to the missionaries as their champions while at the same time insuring respect for

23

the power of Spanish government. Might the sentencing of guilty Acomas have been a ruse to get the Indians to seek missionary help in rescinding the dismemberments? If the missionaries pleaded for the Acomas and were successful in getting the Captain-General to rescind the dismemberments, would the Indians not be more disposed to accept Christianity afterward? It is an historical fact that the Acomas later accepted Christianity.

Could Christianity have been that powerful a force in New Spain in 1599? One must be aware of the role of religion in Spanish society and in the Spanish mind. It can't be overemphasized that Christianization was one of the major goals of Spanish foreign policy. Missionaries and most products of Spanish culture sincerely believed in their religion and considered it the main reason for living. It must be remembered that, in the eyes of the Spanish government, missionaries were as important as the conquistadores themselves. Perhaps a parallel can be drawn for American society: Spaniards of the day believed in Christianity the way many contemporary Americans believe in making money.

In summation we can ask: Is it possible the cutting off of feet after the Acoma War never actually happened? It has already been pointed out that a footless man required to render twenty years of servitude on a farm or ranch would be absolutely ridiculous. It is a fact that Spaniards were meticulous record keepers yet no one at that time ever wrote about having seen a footless Indian at Acoma or anywhere else in New Mexico. Have American writers promoted the dismemberments when in fact it is merely another Black Legend hoax by *Tree of Hate* writers accustomed to denigrating Spain, its people, and its Church? The reader will have to decide.

DISSENSION and DISCONTENT

The summer of 1601 in the New Mexico kingdom on the Río Grande saw the friars and most of the colonists as wanting to abandon the new settlement. Oñate was off exploring the Quivira Country (Kansas) so colonists could debate their frustrations without peril. Where was the grandiose colony they had been promised? Why, even food was hard to come by and starvation would take over if it wasn't for Indian corn and beans! Where were the silver-rich mines that were going to be discovered? Winter temperatures would cause drinking water to freeze in pots on the kitchen table! The land was so poor it couldn't even feed cattle! All this for what, the title of *Hidalgo?!*

In September of 1601 Fr. Francisco de San Miguel advised everyone in church one Sunday that it was their right to abandon the colony if they so desired. He said morality would be on their side because of the injustices that were being inflicted on the Indians, thus preventing their conversion to Christianity, which was the principal reason for colonization.

In early October of 1601, all friars and most of the colonists deserted the colony. Some of the deserters helped themselves to the belongings of the seventy men who were with Oñate, including a number of horses that didn't belong to them. The deserters hit the road and traveled as quickly as their creaking carts would go. They had to make it to the safety of Santa Barbara if they were to be successful.

Only some twenty-five soldiers and their families remained to greet Oñate and his contingent of men when they arrived around November 24, 1601. After the initial shock, Oñate and a military tribunal decided that, after the Captain General had paid all their expenses, the traitors had willfully broken their contract to colonize New Mexico. The leaders were condemned to death by beheading and a troop of soldiers was sent to carry out the sentence and return the others to New Mexico.

But it was too late: the deserters made it to Santa Barbara where Oñate had no jurisdiction. Immediately the deserters set about writing letters to the Viceroy, condemning just about everything Oñate had ever done. This was their main defense because they knew death sentences hung over their heads.[6] (Oñate was going to have to face these charges within a few years. It should be pointed out that Oñate was accused of "cruelty to the Indians" but no one specified that he had ordered the cutting off of 24 Acoma warriors' feet.)

As with archaeological evidence mentioned above, the reader must decide as to the validity of Spanish language documentation. Are Spanish language documents credible? Were Spaniards telling the truth when they recorded what they say they saw or heard? Or were they recording what people of the day wanted to hear? Can Spanish language documentation be the basis for valid history? The reader must decide on this as well as various other assertions promoted by various writers, including that of Oñate's New Mexicans being crypto-Jews.[7]

Documentation for Part II – EURO ENTRADA & SETTLEMENT

1. See Bolton. H.E. *Coronado: Knight of Pueblos and Plains*. Albuquerque: University of New Mexico Press, 1949, pp. 184-8. Bolton's classic work is still considered the best volume on the Coronado expedition.

2. The Gaspar Pérez de Villagrá founding epic, *Historia de la Nueva Mexico,* literally the only epic poem chronicling the founding of any colony in the history of the world, has not been lauded by American writers or society at large. Indeed, the ordinary New Mexican has probably never even read it, perhaps not even part of it since it has not been taught in the public schools.

25

3. Encinias, M., Rodríguez, A., Sánchez, J.P., (editors and translators). *Historia de la Nueva Mexico, 1610.* Albuquerque: University of New Mexico Press, 1992, p. 142.

The only work known to me with a significant discourse on Pueblo homosexuality is that of Ramón Gutiérrez, *When Jesús Came, the Corn Mothers Went Away: Marriage, Sexuality, and Power in New Mexico, 1500-1846.* Stanford: Stanford University Press, 1991, pp. 33-35.

4. Simmons, Marc. *The Last Conquistador: Juan de Oñate and the Settling of the Far Southwest.* Norman: University of Oklahoma Press, 1991, pp. 135-146.

After that of Villagrá, the principal work on the creation of New Mexico is the monumental effort of George Hammond and Agapito Rey titled *Don Juan de Oñate: Colonizer of New Mexico, 1595-1628.* University of New Mexico Press, 1953. See pages 428-479 for the Acoma war.

5. Bancroft, Hubert H. *History of Arizona and New Mexico, 1530-1888.* Albuquerque: Horn & Wallace Publishers, 1962, p. 143.

6. The accusations against Juan de Oñate are with us in American historiography to this day. The context of the charges is not usually included.

7. To my knowledge, Henry J. Tobias and his book *A History of the Jews in New Mexico* (UNM Press, 1990) opened the door to the idea that New Mexican Hispanos might have been "crypto-Jews" during the Spanish colonial period. Villagrá makes no mention of any Jewish connection, neither does Benavides, etc., and neither do historians like J. Manuel Espinosa, Hammond and Rey, John Kessell, Marc Simmons, or David Weber.

Is it possible that crypto-Jews came to New Mexico to escape the Mexican Inquisition? Granted that almost anything is possible in human behavior, Dr. Tobias is the first to admit that it was illegal for non-Christians to come to the New World to begin with. He cites France V. Scholes as stating there was *"very little positive evidence regarding Jews in 17th century New Mexico..."* Then he cites one Fay F. Blake, *"a lay researcher in Albuquerque,"* who asserted *"...there were Jews among the early settlers, but no one admitted it..."* As far-fetched or downright absurd as it seems, the "cloak of secrecy" is somehow an indication that early New Mexican settlers might have been crypto-Jews. In other words, if the settlers didn't admit to being Jewish, they were crypto-Jews.

It is an historical fact that some individuals in New Mexico were accused of being Jews, but they were so accused by their enemies. Investigations by the Inquisition acquitted them of the charge.

Dr. Tobias relates that in 1979 an Hispanic employee of an Albuquerque doctor was wearing a Star of David around her neck. The employee said her mother had instructed her to "return to the old religion." He quotes one

Reverend Symeon Carmona as estimating there could be some 1500 families who are keeping their Jewish origins a secret.

Dr. Tobias concludes his chapter by stating, *"...however tenuous the evidence...the future seems to promise more, not less."* Does that mean more tenuous conjecture or more documented evidence? All of this fantasy is what happens when a group of people loses the power to write its own history.

27

Part III
Background and New Mexico in the 1600s

~

WITCHCRAFT

To understand History one must explore the context of events that were taking place at a specific point in time and, as already indicated, the tendency toward *presentism* must be neutralized. This certainly holds true for the phenomenon of witchcraft, witches, wizards, and trials of witches by church or civil authorities in New Mexico and Europe. As ridiculous as it may seem in the contemporary world, during the 16th and 17th centuries the belief in the existence of witches was ingrained in the people of Europe and those colonists who chose to immigrate to the Americas. Moral authority with which to combat witches supposedly came from Exodus 22:18: *Thou shalt not suffer a witch to live.*

Victims of this persecution, and it has been written four out of five witches were women, number anywhere from 30,000 to the hundreds of thousands in countries like Germany, Switzerland, England, France, and Italy. Sadly, reformers like John Calvin targeted witches as much as any Catholic bishop or inquisitor. While witches were generally portrayed as ugly, in Germany, the sternest country when it came to prosecuting witches, many of the accused and executed were beautiful maidens in the glory of youth.

One might rightly ask if there is a weave of misogyny in the cultures of Germanic northern Europe since the situation can be contrasted by the example of Spain because, according to Marc Simmons, Spain *"…did not succumb to the witch madness…"* It is a documented fact that *"…the Spanish Inquisition loomed as a bulwark of enlightened reason"* against witch mania. He also points out that the activities of the Spanish Inquisition, before and after the witch mania, have been *"…manifestly exaggerated in propaganda disseminated by Spain's enemies."*[1]

It was generally believed that a witch had entered into a pact with the

Devil and in return the witch was given extraordinary powers to inflict harm on anybody. People believed witches could float through the air, pass through walls, etc., to attack helpless victims. They were often blamed for an accident, a sudden illness, bad weather, an insect infestation, etc., as well as disease in domestic animals. They could be blamed for difficulties between husband and wife, impotence, miscarriage, infant death, etc., in short, just about any problem in a community.

Witches and sorcerers were believed to be allied with Satan. They were willing servants, partners in the war against God, Christianity, and goodness in general. As enemies of Christianity the Church took on the responsibility of combating witchcraft.

In European prosecutions four out of five accused witches were *females* and sexual activity was considered a factor in many cases. A witch was considered to be Satan's willing sex slave. The *Prince of Darkness* was portrayed as voracious in his appetite to copulate with Christians who had turned to evil for satisfaction. It was believed Satan could impregnate a young witch in order to bring forth more witches into the world. It was believed that witches held sex orgies when they gathered, copulating with everyone present. In short, the witch was Satan's servant and willing purveyor of evil, an enemy who could destroy even good people living in any village.

All these beliefs could be found in any community, including among the clergy who most often were the intellectual leaders of society. Witchcraft came to be viewed as a threat to Christianity itself. Religious deviance came to be a sign of an all-powerful Satan working his evil wiles on a Christian community.

29

PUEBLO INDIAN Witchcraft

According to archaeologists, when it comes to belief in supernatural powers, Pueblo Indians in New Mexico had a long history dating back to Precontact times. The belief in witches and witchcraft are a part of Pueblo mythology. It is related that folk tales featuring *Coyote, the Trickster,* mention that this entity introduced witchcraft among the people. Coyote married *Yellow Corn Girl* and taught her how to change her form into that of an animal by leaping through a certain ring. There are Pueblo beliefs that a witch can change into a dog, coyote, owl, crow, wolf, bear, rat, deer, cat, or a donkey. Snakes are often considered to be a witch's helper.

While proper ritual and prayer can be used for good, witches and sorcerers who know the secret formulas and procedures can also call upon evil forces. The *cacique,* head priest, represents good, while the witch represents evil. The people believe both are powerful forces in the Pueblo community. Witches are believed to cause illness by stealing the heart of a person or by shooting a foreign object into a person's body. Anyone can be bewitched and the end result is usually death. Witches can create a doll, using deer hide, wool, or cotton, give it the name of the target person, then puncture it with thorns in order to cause serious suffering.

Witches are often motivated by jealousy, a need for revenge, sometimes just plain spite. Children are often special targets for witches, proving how malevolent they really are. Whole families were known to be witches, passing on their black powers to succeeding generations.

Witches have medicine bundles filled with things like shredded rattlesnakes and other nefarious items. They get together at night, often in a cave, to gamble on human hearts, the loser spreading disease amongst villagers so the people will die and give up their hearts. It is believed malevolent witches can destroy an entire village. The people believe a war chief can legally execute a witch by shooting him with arrows.

RELIGION vs. WITCHCRAFT

While the Spaniard also came to the New World to get rich and acquire property, Marc Simmons has written *"...the missionary motive was the most potent and enduring impulse underlying his record of activity in the Americas."* Most Spaniards, starting with Cortés himself, believed that Christianity was a priceless gift for the pagan people of the Americas. To bring aboriginal populations into the Christian fold was the avowed goal of the Spanish Church and State.

Spanish missionaries in New Mexico, products of Spanish European culture, viewed various rituals of the 17th century Pueblo people as pagan rites which did the people great harm. The Indians had many idols, which represented supernatural beings that were viewed by the missionaries as *devil worship*. Missionaries came to the conclusion that medicine men were in reality in league with the Devil, wizards and witches who worked against the Church and the salvation that it offered. In a short time anything disapproved of by the missionaries came to be considered as witchcraft, a concept the Indians themselves understood because they already recognized the existence of witches and the vile things they could do to ordinary people.

CHURCH vs. STATE

Another of the more serious aspects of life in 17th century New Mexico was the constant feuding between church and civil authorities. Much like contemporary Republicans and Democrats, the two groups fought constantly, much of the time over who had final authority over the Indians.

In 1612 Fr. Isidro Ordoñez arrived in New Mexico and lost no time in denouncing Governor Peralta for using unpaid Indian labor to construct

30

government buildings. Further, Ordoñez tells the Christian community that any settler who wishes to leave the colony may do so. Peralta warns that the small colony could be in real peril if settlers decide to leave.

Ordoñez then charges that tribute levied on the Indians is too burdensome, that soldiers are abusing Indian women, that abuses must stop or Governor Peralta will be excommunicated, along with anyone who helps him. Peralta counters that Ordoñez doesn't have the authority to excommunicate anyone so the friar excommunicates the governor. When Peralta decides to go to Mexico City and speak with the Viceroy, Ordoñez and his partisans intercept the governor on the road then keeps him locked up for some nine months.

In 1618 Governor Juan de Eulate announces that the King is the ruler of New Mexico, not the Pope or clergymen in the Church. He informs the Pueblo people that they can perform their ancient rituals with their masks and kachinas. The Franciscans attack him constantly in their correspondence to Mexico City, saying Eulate is *"...more suited to a junk shop than the office of governor which he holds."*

In 1621 Custos Fray Miguel de Chavarría arrives in New Mexico with six new friars. Their orders from the Viceroy himself state they are to *"...conciliate the situation in New Mexico. The friars will cease interfering in civil affairs. The governor will provide military escorts for all missionary activities..."* Heads of Church and State now greet each other in public.

In 1635 the Franciscans charge that sweatshops are being created by civil authorities, including Governor Francisco Martínez de Baeza, that they are involved in illegal ranching operations, that they are monopolizing export items like salt, hides, livestock, and piñon nuts. Civil authorities charge that it is the friars who are doing those things.

In 1637 Governor Luis de Rosas, a no nonsense military man who would knock down any colonist or missionary who got in his way, begins trading with the Indians. The missionaries charge him with enslaving Vaquero Apaches and Utes. (One Nicolás Ortiz stabs Rosas to death in 1642.)

In 1659 Bernardo López de Mendizábal becomes governor. He becomes an active trader, shipping merchandise south. He also decrees that all Indian laborers, including those in missions, must be paid no less than one real per day. The missionaries say they don't have the money so they dismiss their workers. Because Apache raiders have been responsible for the loss of thousands of sheep, the governor then forbids the exportation of sheep. The missionaries ignore the order because sheep are the missions' only source of money with which to pay expenses.

López de Mendizábal permits Indians to perform their ancient dances and rituals. He brings in some dancers from Tesuque and remarks: *"Look*

31

there, this dance contains nothing more than this hu-hu-hu and those thieving friars say it is superstition."

Later he charges the friars with failing to observe their own rules of chastity, poverty, and obedience. The friars counter charge that the governor is a crypto-Jew and is having sexual relations with slaves, an offense punishable under Spanish law by a life sentence to a slave galley. The Inquisition finally steps in: López de Mendizábal is shackled like a common criminal and taken to Mexico City to answer all charges. He dies in prison but after a thorough investigation the Inquisition exonerates him posthumously.

MISSIONARIES vs. MEDICINE MEN

Due to the serious feuds between church and civil authorities, native leaders began to realize that the Christian community was not united. Perhaps this weakness could be used to advantage?

By this time the missionaries were losing patience with the slow progress of Christianization. Aside from ignorant governors, they asserted the medicine men were thwarting the missionizing effort with their black magic and other witcheries. In rare instances of unity, civil authorities used troops to go into the Indian villages, gather up all items used in *devil worship,* and then burn everything in the central plaza. This caused the medicine men to work even harder against the missionaries and their despised Christianity.

The New Mexico missionaries exploited whatever inroads they achieved. For example, Christian behavior dictated the banning of dancing with scalps because they were human body parts, evidence of some bloody, unchristian act. To the Indians, scalps might be viewed as symbols of victory but to the missionaries they were just another tribute to savagery. Christian love would replace chains imposed by the *Devil* and his messengers.

Unlike Europeans, Amerindians had no cultural repulsion to snakes, which were part of some Pueblo traditions and ritual. Medicine men had been observed "talking" to rattlesnakes. Missionaries demanded that Indians stop venerating or dancing with venomous snakes. For example, in the rain dance the dancer held the snake at one end with his mouth, the other with his hand. The snake's undulations were thought to simulate cloud movement, thereby bringing rain. While the missionaries welcomed rain, they didn't believe dancing with snakes could bring it.

As mentioned, snakes had a special place in some Pueblo cultures. A legend associated with the large Pecos Pueblo had it that the medicine men kept a huge serpent in the underground kiva.[2] Not only was the snake of immense size, periodically it had to be fed a newborn child to insure survival of the entire tribe. These steadfast beliefs were cherished especially by the medicine men, who considered themselves defenders of Pueblo tradi-

32

tion and culture. The missionaries fought against what they considered to be *savage* beliefs.

In New Mexico missionaries usually referred to the medicine men as "sorcerers." These native leaders came to resent the Christians and their supposed "holy men," who, incidentally, had also denied them the right to marry several women at the same time. This resentment was understandable for the medicine men had lost their power to the missionaries. Now, in the 1670s, a time of drought, famine, disease, as well as hostile raiders, the native leaders stated it was punishment for allowing missionaries and Christianity into their midst. They promoted the idea that only a return to the old traditions and ways would alleviate their suffering.

DISASTERS

New Mexico was a kingdom filling with disasters before the Pueblo Revolt. The scenario was one of famine caused by drought, disease became a destroyer, and hostile Apache raiders targeted everyone.

In 1669 the Apaches killed six Spanish soldiers and some 373 Christian Indians while they stole upwards of 2000 horses and mules with about as many sheep. At Acoma they took two captives, killed twelve people, and ran off some 800 sheep, 60 cattle, and all the horses the Acomas had.

In 1670 the Apaches of Los Siete Rios went on a total assault against the Salinas pueblos. They attacked the Las Humanas pueblo at harvest time, robbed the church, killed eleven people, and took some 32 captives with them. In time they would destroy six Piro and Salinas pueblos, one of which was Abó.

A horrendous drought had caused a famine suffered by Spanish and Indian communities alike. Hackett quotes that people were reduced to *"eating hides…and roasting them in the fire with maize, and boiling them with herbs and roots."*[3]

In 1671 New Mexico was hit by a pestilence that killed many people and cattle.

In 1672 the Apaches, as hard hit as everyone else, raided all communities, Spanish and Indian, sacking them of many cattle and sheep *"…of which it previously had been very productive."*[4]

Western Apaches swarmed into Zuñi (Hawikuh) in 1673, looting, burning, and killing all who got in their way. The resident missionary Father Avila y Ayala ran into the church and embraced a large cross and a statue of the Blessed Mother. The Apaches dragged him out of the church, tore off all his clothes and threw him down at the foot of a large cross in the plaza. The raiders then shot him full of arrows, stoned him, and finally smashed his head open until the nude, bloody figure at the foot of the cross moved no more.[5]

CRISIS

A real crisis was reached in 1675 when Governor Juan Francisco de Treviño received disturbing reports that the Tewa pueblos were holding *satanic* rites in their kivas, offering grain and other items to the devil. Captain Francisco Javier, the Governor's secretary, was sent out to search for and destroy the *hideous* kachinas masks, idols, and all such items used by native sorcerers in their pacts with Satan.

Further, Treviño had some 47 *sorcerers* rounded up and brought to Santa Fe for trial. Among the charges were bewitching Fr. Andrés Durán of San Ildefonso, of having killed seven other friars and three Spaniards, all by witchcraft. The sorcerers were found guilty: three were hanged, one committed suicide, and the others were whipped.

Javier's destructions and the executions were the last straw. With a sizeable army waiting in the hills outside Santa Fe, some seventy Pueblos went in to see Governor Treviño and demanded the release of their medicine men. They meant business: if their people were not released, the Governor would be killed and Santa Fe attacked. Treviño realized how serious they were and after the exchange of gifts he released the prisoners while asking them to forsake idolatry.

Documentation for BACKGROUND and NEW MEXICO in the 1600s

1. Simmons, Marc. *Witchcraft in the Southwest: Spanish and Indian Supernaturalism on the Río Grande.* Lincoln: University of Nebraska Press, 1980, pp. 7-15.

Simmons is correct in his observation. For example, while most people have heard about the Inquisitor of the Inquisition, who could discuss the *Witch Finder General* of northern Europe and the American colonies?

For Simmons' chapter on "Pueblo Witchcraft," see pp. 69-95.

For a general work on European witchery see *Servants of Satan* by Joseph Klaits.

2. Kessell, John L. Kiva, Cross, & Crown. Tucson: Southwest Parks and Monuments Association, ©?; UNM reprint 1987, pp. 472-73.

3. Hackett, C.W. *Revolt of the Pueblo Indians of New Mexico and Otermín's Attempted Reconquest, 1680-1682.* Albuquerque: University of New Mexico Press, 1942, p. xix, passim. (Dr. Charmion Clair Shelby did the translation of Spanish language documents.)

This statement has always been a curiosity. Roasted (?) cowhides might be chewy but how much nutrition do they contain? Were cowhides saved up somewhere in order to be available for later eating during a famine? How long can a human being survive on a diet of roasted/boiled cowhide? What happened to the meat the cowhide used to contain? Where were all the sheep? Is this information more hyperbole than actual historical fact?

4. This contradicts the "eating hides" statement above, unless one believes disappeared cattle and sheep could make a significant comeback in two years.

5. *Kiva, Cross, & Crown,* p. 216.

Part IV
The Plan
~
Po'pay

O NE OF THOSE WHO HAD BEEN WHIPPED BUT NOW RELEASED by Governor Treviño was Po'pay (which has been translated as *Ripe Squash* or *Ripe Pumpkin* or *Ripe Cultigens*) from San Juan Pueblo. It is said that from the moment of his release, Po'pay went to Taos, the northern most pueblo, and began to plan a revolution against the Spaniards, their missionaries, and their Christianity.

From the time of his appearance into the historical record in 1675, Po'pay was and continues to be an enigma. Further, what little that is known comes from Spanish language documents. There is no archaeological information on the leader, and especially astounding, there is no Pueblo oral history on this principal personality of the Revolt.

According to the venerable Joe Sando, "...*oral history passed down...*" from the time of Coronado is still a part of Pueblo oral history traditions. [1] With Coronado operating in New Mexico from 1540 to 1542 and Po'pay from 1675 to around 1688, why would there be no strong oral history on the leader of this *"first American revolution"*? There has been no answer to this question.

What did Po'pay look like? Was he tall? Short? Was he a medicine man? A war chief? Married or unmarried? Did he have children? Did he have a house in San Juan? Was he a typical village farmer? Did he trade with eastern Apache groups? Were his parents from San Juan or did he have blood ties to other pueblos? If that is where he made his new home, how was he accepted at Taos? What was his reputation around the New Mexico pueblos? Pueblo oral history does not tell us, at least not from well known Pueblo voices like Joe Sando, Herman Agoyo, Alfonso Ortiz, etc., who would certainly know if such oral history, *"remembering by the eyes and ears,"* existed.

To unite the different Amerindian villages of New Mexico would have

36

to be considered a daunting task. It appears Po'pay and other leaders were equal to the task. Leaders included Luis and Lorenzo Tupatú from Picurís, Antonio Malacate from Cochití, Francisco El Ollita from San Ildefonso, Antonio Bolsas from Santa Fe, Cristóbal Yope from San Lázaro, Alonzo Catiti from Santo Domingo, El Jaca (Saca?) from Taos. Mixed bloods like Domingo Naranjo of Santa Clara, Domingo Romero from Tesuque, and Nicolás Jonva from San Ildefonso were permitted in the group. Pent up resentment and downright rage were carefully controlled but somehow communicated to most pueblos that the Spanish and their Christian God could be defeated.

Over the years the revolutionaries would meet secretly, especially during a village feast day, so as not to arouse suspicion. Amazingly, the plan remained a well-kept secret almost until the uprising itself.

Inspired by the Pueblo god *Poheyemo,* a bold strategy was agreed to by Po'pay and his partisans: *death* to all missionaries, Spanish Christians, and "wethead" (Christian) Indians who helped them. There would be no exceptions if harmony and prosperity were to return to the land. *The time would come for all Pueblo people to destroy the Spanish oppressors who had taken away their kachinas, their kivas, their wives, and their rituals.* Soon word would be sent. Preparations must be made, but secretly.

37

PRELUDE

By 1676 New Mexico was once again on the brink of extinction due to the drought and raiding hostiles. Custodio Father Francisco Ayeta was in Mexico City pleading for assistance, asking for at least 50 professional soldiers and 1,000 horses to accompany his supply-laden caravan for his return to New Mexico. He was successful and made his way back to the province in 1677 with a new Governor, Antonio de Otermín.

By September of 1678 the energetic Father Ayeta was back in Mexico City asking for more help. He also asked that a presidio be created in Santa Fe with 50 professional soldiers to man it. Then he headed back north to New Mexico and was scheduled to arrive in September of 1680.

Po'pay and the other leaders knew they must strike before the supply caravan returned from Mexico City. *Secrecy* was still crucial. When Po'pay's son-in-law, Nicolas Bua, refused to join the rebellion, indicating he would inform the Spanish authorities, Po'pay had him murdered.

Word was sent out by the means of knotted cords that August 13 would be the date for a general uprising. And messengers let it be known that any pueblo that did not join the revolt would be exterminated right along with the Christians.

Governor Otermín is informed by friendly caciques that a bloody uprising would burst forth on August 13.

Two men from Tesuque, Nicolás Catua and Pedro Omtua, are found with knotted cords, arrested, and taken to Santa Fe for interrogation. *Po'pay realizes his plan has been discovered* so he quickly puts out the word that August 10 is the day to rise up and destroy the hated Christians. He assured the warriors that all who killed a Spaniard would get a woman for a wife, kill four Spaniards and you get four, *kill ten and you get ten women.* He lets it be known that Apaches will also be fighting the Spaniards.

POPULATION of NEW MEXICO in 1680

How many Hispanics were in New Mexico on the eve of the Revolt? H.H. Bancroft estimates the number at about 2400. France Scholes has written the Spanish population never exceeded 2500. Hackett states there were some 2800 Spanish inhabitants in New Mexico. Whatever the exact number, most of the population lived in outlying farms and ranches, making their living by stock raising and intensive agriculture. More settlers lived in the Río Abajo area than around Santa Fe, the only villa in New Mexico.

Antonio de Otermín was the Governor and Captain-General in 1680. There was no presidio but there were some professional soldiers in Santa Fe. Alonso García was Lieutenant Governor for the Río Abajo. There were thirty-two (32) Franciscan missionaries serving throughout the province. There were some 16,000 Christianized Indians before the Revolt. Christian inroads hadn't been made with Apaches or Navajos.

Documentation for PART IV – THE PLAN

1. Sando, Joe and Agoyo, Herman (eds.) *Po'pay: Leader of the First American Revolution.* Santa Fe: Clear Light Publishing, 2005, p. 11.

In pages 5-53 historian Sando gives a short history of the Pueblo Revolt, which is reviewed below. When talking about Po'pay, Dr. Sando makes general statements like *"...There is no reason to believe he did not grow up like any other Pueblo Indian boy of his time, strictly following the rules and rhythms of the community."* He also provides (p. 24) what he calls *"an imaginative recreation"* of how the Revolt was planned.

Part V
The St. Lawrence Day Massacre
~

I N THE EARLY MORNING OF AUGUST 10, FATHER JUAN PÍO WALKS to the village of Tesuque to say mass. A soldier named Pedro Hidalgo accompanies him. When the two get to Tesuque they find the village empty. When he encounters the villagers they are heavily armed and wearing war paint. *"What is this, are you mad?"* asks Fr. Pío. *"Do not disturb yourselves. I will help you and die a thousand deaths for you."* He is immediately dragged away to a nearby ravine and bludgeoned to death while other warriors go after the soldier Pedro Hidalgo. Hidalgo strikes back at the men trying to unseat him while hanging on to the horse from all sides. He spurs the animal, dragging the warriors along until they fall to the ground. Hidalgo makes it to Santa Fe and lets his superiors know what has happened, that Fr. Pío is most certainly dead.

Bands of Pueblo Indians everywhere attack Hispanic Christians wherever found, shooting them with arrows or splitting their heads open with war clubs. Not knowing of the uprising, most Hispanics in outlying farms and ranches were not prepared to defend themselves so men, women, and children are killed in the savage onslaught. There is no mercy for anyone, not even young children or babes in arms who fall with their skulls bashed in. *The unsuspecting Christians are sent to their Christian god so hated by the Indians.* The slaughter is horrific despite the screams of women and piercing cries of children. The victorious marauders take anything of value, especially weapons and horses, and then set fire to all buildings. Hispanic New Mexico is being drenched in blood then going up in smoke.

The hated friars are special targets for the rampaging Indians. Most are killed immediately but some are kept alive momentarily to be tortured. At Jémez Pueblo Father Juan de Jesús is captured and told that this night he is going to be inducted into knighthood. His clothes are torn off him then

39

he is paraded to the cemetery where many candles are lit as in a solemn Christian ceremony. Since every knight must have a gallant steed Fr. Juan is forced to mount a pig. He is taunted with *Where is your Jesús god now? Why doesn't your St. James come and save you, Reverend Father?!* Finally he is kicked off the pig and forced to get on all fours after which the warriors mount him and ride him around the cemetery, whipping him all the while. Father Juan finally tells them *"Do with me as you wish for this joy of yours will not last and in ten years you will consume each other."* This enflames the warriors even more because Father Juan will not break and beg for mercy. From all sides they attack him with war clubs until his face is so bloody it is unrecognizable. Having done away with a priest the gleeful warriors now leave to find more Christians.

At Acoma Father Lucas Maldonado and Father Juan de Val are taken prisoner, along with an elderly Christian mestiza named Juana Maroh (who would turn out being the grandmother of the later famous Keres war captain Bartolomé de Ojeda). The Acomas strip all three of their clothes then tie them together with a rope, the female between the two priests. The three are paraded around the village, taunted by all who see them, and whipped while they walk. The warriors stop them at the church entrance and invite all Acomas to stone the three Christian figures. Many Acomas hurl rocks at the trio until they fall to the ground. The victorious warriors then take turns lancing them where they lay until they are dead. Finally the jubilant Acomas drag the bodies around the village and eventually toss them in the garbage pit.

Some Hispanos from the Río Arriba jurisdiction are able to fight their way to safety in Santa Fe. Everyone is under attack but no one is really aware of the extent of the carnage. Word gets out that Los Cerrillos villagers, led by Sergeant Major Bernabé Márquez, are under siege so a squad of soldiers is sent out to rescue them, successfully.

Hispanos from Río Abajo, led by Alonso García, congregate at Isleta Pueblo. Isleta had not joined the general rebellion but messengers from the warring tribes were encouraging them to do so by killing all Christians in their midst.

By August 13 Santa Fe is under siege but the only undestroyed settlement in Río Arriba. There are perhaps a thousand people gathered in the villa with fewer than a hundred men capable of bearing arms. The rest are mostly women and children who constantly hear blood-curdling war cries and menacing chants coming from the hostiles.

The Indians, now including Apaches, appear to number in the thousands. Some are on horseback and carrying harquebusiers taken from dead Christians. Governor Otermín asks for a parley in which he asks for peace

40

"...and you will be pardoned." Juan, one of the Indian leaders who was riding horseback and carrying an harquebus, sword, and dagger, informs Otermín that the Spaniards must leave the country or all will be killed as they have been throughout the province. Two painted crosses are offered to the governor: a red one for war, a white one for leaving New Mexico. Otermín rejects both crosses and Juan returns to the Indian lines amid great war yells, the ringing of bells, and the burning of the chapel of San Miguel.

Meanwhile, the refugees at Isleta receive word that all settlers in the Río Arriba have been killed. Alonso García asks the people what they wish to do and the vote is to make their way to El Paso, since everyone up north is already dead. García leads the people south in accordance with their unanimous vote. A number of Christian Isleta Indians go with them because they realize they will be killed by the forces of Po'pay for becoming Christians.

By August 20 the Santa Fe water supply has been cut off and there is a real possibility of dying of thirst. The Indians fight their way closer and closer, so close they can be heard taunting the Christians: *Your god is dead!! The god who was your father is dead!! Mary who is your mother and your saints are pieces of rotten wood!!!*

The Spaniards decide there is no choice but to go out of the villa and attack the Indian besiegers. There were fewer than a hundred fighting men and some had to be left behind for defense but the Spanish realized all would perish if their charge wasn't successful. Invoking the name of *Santa María* the Spaniards rush at the surprised Indians, the horses trampling over some of the scurrying warriors, dislodging them from the streets and houses they had been holding.

The Indians regrouped, many armed with Spanish weapons taken from dead settlers, engaged their Christian enemies at the outskirts of the settlement and fought like tigers. Despite their small numbers, the Spaniards fight with sterling Christian courage and intensity, driving the warriors back, only to encounter more Indians coming to join the fight. Governor Otermín then came out of the villa with reinforcements and the tide turned once again. The battle raged all day, sometimes hand-to-hand, Spanish steel and resolve pitted against overwhelming numbers. By evening the Spaniards were once more on the verge of victory when warriors from the Tewa, Taos, and Picurís arrived on the scene. Concerned that so many Indians coming to battle might attack the refugees in the villa, the Spanish fighters retreat to find that houses and the church were indeed being set on fire. More warriors were seen gathering, seemingly from every direction. There could have been as many as 5000 warriors getting ready for the final kill.

Pecos warriors, unable to win against Spanish fighting men, now went to their village and slaughtered the Spanish women who had previously been taken captive.

Marauding avengers on unsuspecting farm and ranch families living mostly in isolated locales had waged previous attacks. The fight for Santa Fe was the only real battle of the Revolt. It is written that some 300 Indians were killed and that five Spaniards died during the battle. In customary Spanish style, the defeat and rout of the attackers was considered miraculous for the overwhelming numbers of Indians, some riding horses and armed with European weapons, might well have annihilated the small band of Christian defenders.

Governor Otermín now questioned the prisoners taken during the battle, some 47 in number, and learned the entire country from Taos to Isleta had been devastated. All the Christians in the area had been slain. *Everyone!!* The only ones left were those in Santa Fe and they had a death sentence on them, which would come soon. Otermín had all the prisoners executed.

The governor realized his people could not survive in Santa Fe. It would have to be abandoned. He gave the order for everyone to prepare to travel south toward Isleta where perhaps survivors from the Río Abajo would be waiting for his people from the Río Arriba.

The caravan of refugees, overwhelmingly women and children, made its slow way out of Santa Fe, Indians watching them from all sides. Soldiers were placed protectively on each side of the caravan, front and rear. Even the women were ready to fight if an attack came. An all out attack by the Indians certainly would have annihilated the small group of Spanish Christians. But the Indians had now engaged Spanish fighting men, no longer unsuspecting settlers, so they let the refugees pass without attacking them.

The Christians realized an ambush could be staged at any suitable point in the road so the tension continued to build. Indians and their smoke signals were seen throughout the retreat. For whatever reasons, the Indians did not attack. Perhaps the Pueblos now understood they had accomplished their goal. The hated oppressors were leaving the country and everything foreign could be destroyed.

Churches became special targets. Images and statues considered *holy representations* by the hated Spaniards were hacked to pieces. Altars were urinated on and reduced to rubble. Sacramental chalices were used for defecation. Priest vestments were torn to shreds. Holes were hacked in church roofs and fires were set to burn everything down. In some places even the walls were razed to the ground, such was the virulent hatred toward Christianity.

The devastation throughout New Mexico was indeed horrific and the caravan of refugees was able to witness some of it as it made its way south. Houses had been ransacked then burned. The same with churches. Bodies of Hispano settlers and those of priests were encountered along the way. Some showed signs of torture. Below San Felipe Pueblo at the estancia of Sergeant Major Cristóbal de Anaya were found the naked bodies of twelve persons, including Anaya himself, Leonor his wife, three children, and two soldiers. Further down the house of Pedro de Cuellar had been sacked then destroyed. Yet further on the road was the house of Captain Augustín de Carbajal, which had also been robbed. The bodies of Carbajal, his wife Damiana, their daughter, and another woman had been stripped of all clothing then left on the floor.

Refugees went into further shock. They had never seen such destruction, even in this isolated outpost of Christendom. The caravan of refugees stopped to bury the bodies they encountered.

At Sandía Pueblo a large group of hostiles were sighted, shouting and daring the Spaniards to fight. Some were mounted, some had harquebusiers. Governor Otermín sent a squad of some 50 soldiers to engage the Indians, who promptly fled to the mountains. The Indians had burned the church so in retaliation Otermín ordered that the pueblo be burned, which was done.

When the caravan arrived at Isleta Pueblo there wasn't a living soul to be found. Otermín had hoped Alonso García and his people would be waiting for the Río Arriba group. *Where was García?! Why had he abandoned his jurisdiction?! Had he deserted with the soldiers so sorely needed up north?!* Perhaps he had made it to safety in the south? *He had no authority to leave!* Riders were sent out to find him.

On September 6 Alonso García was brought into Otermín's camp at La Salineta. The governor immediately placed him under arrest. During the court martial Alonso García was given ample opportunity to explain his actions. Since the Lieutenant General had kept detailed records of everything that happened, the governor later concluded that García had acted correctly, considering the circumstances. All charges were dropped. García expressed his gratitude for the justice and understanding with which he had been treated.

The two groups now united, the refugees continued their journey south. Just before getting to El Paso, the New Mexican caravan met Father Ayeta and his supply wagons on September 18. The people could finally eat something besides corn. Father Ayeta was hailed as a savior for indeed that is what he was to the shattered pioneers. The people were now able to make it to El Paso where they were required to settle.

CASUALTIES

Following is a partial list of people who were killed, "captured or carried off," or turned up missing after the massacre. [1]

43

TAOS Pueblo: Captain Marcos de las Heras, Alcalde Mayor of Taos.
TAOS Pueblo: Elena, wife of Major Fernando Durán y Chaves;
TAOS Pueblo: son [1] of Elena and Fernando Durán y Chaves;
TAOS Pueblo: child [2] of Elena and Fernando Durán y Chaves;
TAOS Pueblo: child [3] of Elena and Fernando Durán y Chaves;
TAOS Pueblo: child [4] of Elena and Fernando Durán y Chaves;

TAOS Pueblo: unnamed Christian woman;
TAOS Pueblo: Maria, wife of Domingo de Herrera;
TAOS Pueblo: child [1] of María and Domingo de Herrera;
TAOS Pueblo: child [2] of María and Domingo de Herrera;
TAOS Pueblo: child [3] of María and Domingo de Herrera;
TAOS Pueblo: child [4] of María and Domingo de Herrera;
TAOS Pueblo: child [5] of María and Domingo de Herrera;
TAOS Pueblo: child [6] of María and Domingo de Herrera;
TAOS Pueblo: child [7] of María and Domingo de Herrera;

TAOS Pueblo: Major Sebastián de Herrera;
TAOS Pueblo: Juana, wife of Sebastián de Herrera;
TAOS Pueblo: Ana Baca, mother of Juana;
TAOS Pueblo: brother of Juana;

TAOS Pueblo: mother of María Ramos;
TAOS Pueblo: brother [1] of María Ramos;
TAOS Pueblo: brother [2] of María Ramos;

TAOS Pueblo: mother of Colonel Diego Lucero de Godoy;
TAOS Pueblo: sister [1] of Colonel Diego Lucero de Godoy;
TAOS Pueblo: sister [2] of Colonel Diego Lucero de Godoy;
TAOS Pueblo: sister [3] of Colonel Diego Lucero de Godoy;

TAOS Pueblo: Father Antonio de Mora;
TAOS Pueblo: Father Matías Rendón;
TAOS Pueblo: Father Antonio Sanchez de Pío;

PICURÍS Pueblo: Francisco Blanco de la Vega;
PICURÍS Pueblo: female mulato slave of Francisco Xavier;
PICURÍS Pueblo: son of female mulato slave of Francisco Xavier;

TAOS & PICURÍS Pueblos: member [1] of soldier family;
TAOS & PICURÍS Pueblos: member [2] of soldier family;

TAOS & PICURÍS Pueblos: member [3] of soldier family;
TAOS & PICURÍS Pueblos: member [4] of soldier family;
TAOS & PICURÍS Pueblos: member [5] of soldier family;
TAOS & PICURÍS Pueblos: member [6] of soldier family;
TAOS & PICURÍS Pueblos: member [7] of soldier family;
TAOS & PICURÍS Pueblos: member [8] of soldier family;
TAOS & PICURÍS Pueblos: member [9] of soldier family;
TAOS & PICURÍS Pueblos: member [10] of soldier family;
TAOS & PICURÍS Pueblos: member [11] of soldier family;
TAOS & PICURÍS Pueblos: member [12] of soldier family;
TAOS & PICURÍS Pueblos: member [13] of soldier family;
TAOS & PICURÍS Pueblos: member [14] of soldier family;
TAOS & PICURÍS Pueblos: member [15] of soldier family;
TAOS & PICURÍS Pueblos: member [16] of soldier family;
TAOS & PICURÍS Pueblos: member [17] of soldier family;
TAOS & PICURÍS Pueblos: member [18] of soldier family;
TAOS & PICURÍS Pueblos: member [19] of soldier family;
TAOS & PICURÍS Pueblos: member [20] of soldier family;
TAOS & PICURÍS Pueblos: member [21] of soldier family;
TAOS & PICURÍS Pueblos: member [22] of soldier family;
TAOS & PICURÍS Pueblos: member [23] of soldier family;
TAOS & PICURÍS Pueblos: member [24] of soldier family;
TAOS & PICURÍS Pueblos: member [25] of soldier family;
TAOS & PICURÍS Pueblos: member [26] of soldier family;
TAOS & PICURÍS Pueblos: member [27] of soldier family;
TAOS & PICURÍS Pueblos: member [28] of soldier family;
TAOS & PICURÍS Pueblos: member [29] of soldier family;
TAOS & PICURÍS Pueblos: member [30] of soldier family;
TAOS & PICURÍS Pueblos: member [31] of soldier family;

TESUQUE Pueblo: Cristóbal de Herrera [youth];
TESUQUE Pueblo: Father Juan Bautista Pío;

POJOAQUE Pueblo: Captain Francisco Jiménez;
POJOAQUE Pueblo: wife of Captain Francisco Jiménez;
POJOAQUE Pueblo: entire family of Captain Francisco Jiménez;

POJOAQUE Pueblo: Joseph de Goitia;
POJOAQUE Pueblo: Petronila de Salas (wife or widow of Pedro Romero);
POJOAQUE Pueblo: grown son [1] of Petronila de Salas;
POJOAQUE Pueblo: grown son [2] of Petronila de Salas;

45

POJOAQUE Pueblo: grown son [3] of Petronila de Salas;
POJOAQUE Pueblo: grown daughter [4] of Petronila de Salas;
POJOAQUE Pueblo: grown daughter [5] of Petronila de Salas;
POJOAQUE Pueblo: child [6] of Petronila de Salas;
POJOAQUE Pueblo: child [7] of Petronila de Salas;
POJOAQUE Pueblo: child [8] of Petronila de Salas;
POJOAQUE Pueblo: child [9] of Petronila de Salas;
POJOAQUE Pueblo: child [10] of Petronila de Salas;

SANTA CLARA Pueblo: soldier Felipe López;
SANTA CLARA Pueblo: soldier Marcos Ramos;
SANTA CLARA Pueblo: Francisca, wife of Francisco de Anaya;
SANTA CLARA Pueblo: all the children of Francisca and Francisco Anaya;
NAMBÉ Pueblo: Sebastián de Torres;
NAMBÉ Pueblo: wife of Sebastián de Torres;
NAMBÉ Pueblo: child of Sebastián de Torres;
NAMBÉ Pueblo: Father Tomás de Torres;

SANTO DOMINGO Pueblo: Major Andrés de Peralta;
46 SANTO DOMINGO Pueblo: soldier [1] at Santo Domingo;
SANTO DOMINGO Pueblo: soldier [2] at Santo Domingo;
SANTO DOMINGO Pueblo: soldier [3] at Santo Domingo;
SANTO DOMINGO Pueblo: soldier [4] at Santo Domingo;

SANTO DOMINGO Pueblo: civilian [1] on Santo Domingo road;
SANTO DOMINGO Pueblo: civilian [2] on Santo Domingo road;
SANTO DOMINGO Pueblo: civilian [3] on Santo Domingo road;
SANTO DOMINGO Pueblo: civilian [4] on Santo Domingo road;
SANTO DOMINGO Pueblo: civilian [5] on Santo Domingo road;
SANTO DOMINGO Pueblo: civilian [6] on Santo Domingo road;

SANTO DOMINGO Pueblo: Father Juan de Talabán;
SANTO DOMINGO Pueblo: Father Francisco Antonio Lorenzana
SANTO DOMINGO Pueblo: Father Josep0h de Montes de Oca;

SANTA FE: Colonel Andres Gómez Robledo;
SANTA FE: soldier Lucas de Gamboa;
SANTA FE: unidentified soldier [1];
SANTA FE: unidentified soldier [2];
SANTA FE: unidentified soldier [3];

SANTA FE: unidentified soldier [4];

GALISTEO: Juan de Leiva, assistant Alcalde Mayor;
GALISTEO: Nicolas de Leiva;

GALISTEO: Catalina, wife of Maestre de Campo Pedro de Leiva;
GALISTEO: Dorotea de Leiva, daughter [1] of Pedro de Leiva;;
GALISTEO: daughter [2] of Pedro de Leiva;

GALISTEO: Juana Fresqui;
GALISTEO: child of Juana Fresqui;

GALISTEO: Lázaro García de Noriega;
GALISTEO: Francisco de Anaya Almazán III;

GALISTEO: Captain Joseph Nieto;
GALISTEO: wife of Captain Joseph Nieto;
GALISTEO: daughter [1] of Joseph Nieto;
GALISTEO: daughter [2] of Joseph Nieto;

GALISTEO: Father Domingo d Vera;
GALISTEO: Father Juan Bernal;

PECOS Pueblo: Spanish female [1] captive;
PECOS Pueblo: Spanish female [2] captive;
PECOS Pueblo: Spanish child [3] captive;
PECOS Pueblo: Spanish child [4] captive;
PECOS Pueblo: Spanish child [5] captive;

PECOS Pueblo: Father Juan de la Pedrosa;
PECOS Pueblo: Father Fernando de Velasco;

SAN ILDEFONSO Pueblo: Father Luis de Morales;

ANGOSTURA: Captain Agustín de Carvajal;
ANGOSTURA: grown daughter of Agustín de Carvajal;
ANGOSTURA: woman in household of Agustín de Carvajal;

ANGOSTURA: Damiana Domínguez de Mendoza;
ANGOSTURA: Captain Cristóbal de Anaya;
ANGOSTURA: Leonor, wife of Cristóbal de Anaya;

ANGOSTURA: grown daughter [1] of Cristóbal de Anaya;
ANGOSTURA: grown daughter [2] of Cristóbal de Anaya;
ANGOSTURA: child [3] of Cristóbal de Anaya;
ANGOSTURA: child [4] of Cristóbal de Anaya;
ANGOSTURA: grown son [5] of Cristóbal de Anaya;
ANGOSTURA: grown son [6] of Cristóbal de Anaya;
ANGOSTURA: household member [7] of Cristóbal de Anaya;
ANGOSTURA: household member [8] of Cristóbal de Anaya;
ANGOSTURA: household member [9] of Cristóbal de Anaya;
ANGOSTURA: household member [10] of Cristóbal de Anaya;

ANGOSTURA: wife of Pedro de Cuellar;
ANGOSTURA: child of Pedro de Cuellar;

RÍO ABAJO: wife of Antonio Lucero de Godoy;
RÍO ABAJO: child [1] of Antonio Lucero de Godoy;
RÍO ABAJO: child [2] of Antonio Lucero de Godoy;

RÍO ABAJO: wife of Francisco Varela;
RÍO ABAJO: nephew [1] of Catalina Zamora Lucero;
RÍO ABAJO: nephew [2] of Catalina Zamora Lucero;

RÍO ABAJO: son-in-law [1] of Inez Luz;
RÍO ABAJO: son-in-law [2] of Inez Luz;

RÍO ABAJO: Cristóbal Durán y Chávez;
RÍO ABAJO: wife of Cristóbal Durán y Chávez;
RÍO ABAJO: child [1] of Cristóbal Durán y Chávez;
RÍO ABAJO: child [2] of Cristóbal Durán y Chávez;
RÍO ABAJO: child [3] of Cristóbal Durán y Chávez;
RÍO ABAJO: child [4] of Cristóbal Durán y Chávez;
RÍO ABAJO: child [5] of Cristóbal Durán y Chávez;

RÍO ABAJO—Jémez Pueblo: Father Juan de Jesús;
RÍO ABAJO—Acoma Pueblo: Father Lucas Maldonado;

Servants were also targeted by the rampaging revolutionaries of August 10. Some seventy-seven (77) servants were identified as "killed, captured, or missing" after the massacre, the largest numbers listed as follows: Major Fernando Durán y Chaves reported twenty-eight (28) servants in those categories; Colonel Pedro de Leyva reported twenty-seven (27); Major Diego

Lucero de Godoy reported twenty (20); etc. Servants who were Indian were targeted right along with those who weren't.

It is impossible to provide exact figures for the loss of life during the St. Lawrence Day Massacre. The best that can be done is an approximation. It was reported that seventy-three (73) Spanish men of military age lost their lives during the massacre. Twenty-one (21) priests were martyred. The official death count in 1680 was therefore set at 401 so it is logical to assume that some 300-plus deaths were of noncombatant women and children.

The news rocked the Spanish Empire. *Perhaps as much as 15% of the whole New Mexican colony had been slaughtered. Nowhere in the entire Spanish Empire had aboriginal people ever taken back a province before it happened in New Mexico.*

It turned out that some twenty-one (21) Spanish women and around thirty-nine (39) Indian/mestizos were taken captive and not killed by their captors, which would lower the overall death count to about 341 (if the Indian/mestizo servants number was included among the Spanish dead). It would still hold that about 75% of those killed on or around St. Lawrence Day were noncombatant women and children.

It is recorded that nine (9) children were born to various captive females during their twelve-year captivity.

49

Twelve-Year INTERREGNUM

The hated Christian oppressors were finally *gone!* The Pueblo people could once again live their lives in freedom, practicing the ways of their ancestors and traveling the corn pollen trail. They could enjoy their families, the gifts of nature, etc., and be one with all creation. It was a time to *dance!* Life would continue in harmony as soon as everything Spanish was discarded.

So did the Pueblo people get rid of their horses, their cows, their sheep, their fruit trees, etc., their *chile* and *squash blossom jewelry* brought by the oppressive Spaniards? Did the liberated people throw out steel tools, swords, knives, and their newly acquired harquebusiers? Once again, Pueblo oral history doesn't relate what happened during these twelve years. One thing is certain: shedding missionary blood proved futile when it came to bringing clouds full of rain. Replacing Christianity with ancient Pueblo rituals did not end the drought for it continued its destructive reign, despite the snake writhing rain dance.

Killing as many Hispanic people as possible did not bring unity to Pueblo land. Once more Amerindian society became Pueblo groups against other Pueblo groups. Worse still, Apache and Navajo raiders were targeting all villages for their livestock and crops. *The Apaches had been accepted as allies against the Spanish oppressors but now they were the enemy, again!* And they showed no mercy against the liberated Pueblo people and their rein-stated ancient rituals. *Pueblo extermination was now quite possible at the hands of hostile Indians.* Pueblo oral history doesn't provide details but the threat was very real.

Neither does oral history relate what happened to the leader Po'pay because within a relatively short time he was deposed/replaced by Luis Tupatú from Picurís Pueblo.[2] This is known only because people writing in the Spanish language recorded it. Did Po'pay indeed become a tyrant, worse than the tyrannical Spanish governors and missionaries? Did he really go around in a horse and buggy, despite ordering everyone else to destroy everything Spanish? The answers remain unknown.

It is related that in July of 1683, Luis Tupatú sent a messenger, one Juan Punsilli, to negotiate with the Spaniards about coming back to northern New Mexico. The message was that if Spaniards would return, Luis Tupatú would help if the Christians didn't exact revenge. Some expeditions would be sent but it would take the appearance of a great leader to recolonize the province.

Documentation for PART V – The ST LAWRENCE DAY MASSACRE

1. These figures are mostly from Hackett's monumental volumes. Luis Brandtner did a study of these numbers that were published in *HERENCIA: The Quarterly Journal of the Hispanic Genealogical Research Center of New Mexico,* Volume 7, Issues 2 and 4, April and October 1999.

2. *PO'PAY,* p. 39-41.

Part VI
Diego de Vargas

D IEGO JOSÉ DE VARGAS ZAPATA Y LUJÁN PONCE DE LEÓN Y Contreras was born in Madrid, Spain, in 1643. His family belonged to the middle ranking nobility of Madrid but his ancestors had been warrior knights, bishops, friends of the saints, and advisors to kings. Four generations of Vargas men, including Diego's father, were knights in the Military Order of Santiago.

Diego arrives in the New World in 1673, his wife in Spain dies in 1674. By 1679 Diego has a government post in the silver-rich district of Tlalpujahua. He is recommended for higher office and is eventually appointed to the governorship of New Mexico in 1687. Due to circumstances beyond his control he doesn't journey north until five years later in 1692. He vows he will return the Christian colony to New Mexico and will not exterminate the Pueblo Indians in the process.

Vargas arrives in El Paso in February of 1692. He finds the settlers in terrible condition. There are some 100 families with maybe 200 horses and mules, no cattle, and perhaps 600 sheep, owned mostly by the missionaries. Soldiers don't have leather jackets or swords and they own maybe 132 horses. Immediately he requests modern muskets and other war materiel while he makes plans for an armed reconnaissance into the north.

On August 16, 1692, Roque de Madrid leads his reconnaissance force to a camp known as *Robledo* where Vargas arrives later with the rest of the expeditionary force. In all the force includes some 50 presidial soldiers and their officers, 10 fully armed citizens, perhaps 100 tough Pueblo warriors, and 3 Franciscans. The group is small for the task ahead but Vargas is considered an effective leader because he can relate to Hispanos, Indians, mestizos, blacks, etc., who make up colonial society.

On September 11 Vargas enters Santa Fe unopposed. In a few days he meets with Luis and Lorenzo Tupatú, brothers from Picurís. They confer, along with the missionary fathers, over cups of hot chocolate. The Tupatús are given full pardons for their role in the massacre of 1680. They become allies of Vargas and his Christians.

On September 21 Vargas takes an expeditionary force, which includes 300 Tupatú-led warriors from Picurís, against the very large Pecos Pueblo. The Pecos people and their chieftain, Juan de Ye, welcome Vargas peacefully. It appears the Pecos desire peace.

Vargas goes up to Taos then to pueblos down the Río Grande corridor then to the west. Though he has only around 89 soldiers and some 30 Indian allies there is no resistance. Rumors abound about who is getting ready to fight but there is no battle anywhere and it appears the Pueblo people sincerely desire peace. Amazingly, some people thought to have been killed in the massacre are found alive and freed from their captivity.

Vargas is elated with this bloodless Reconquest of New Mexico's 23 pueblos comprising so many different nations. He reports that the province now needs around 500 Christian Hispanic families and no less than 100 professional soldiers to secure the bloodless Reconquest.

Vargas COLONISTS

Vargas had previously conducted an El Paso census to determine the number of colonists available for recolonizing New Mexico. The survey turned up some 959 individuals in 112 households. There were 73 married couples, 115 widows/widowers/singles. There were 448 boys and girls. There were some nineteen Mexican Indian households, which were probably recorded in the census with about 250 servants. All these people were survivors of the Pueblo Revolt and the twelve years of poverty and deprivation in El Paso.

The new settlers recruited from Mexico City and Puebla to go to New Mexico with Vargas have been described as *"a colony of cousins."*[1] Fathers and their sons, brothers and their sisters and their cousins living in Mexico City and neighboring Puebla enrolled for life in New Mexico.

By and large, the settler who went to New Mexico was listed as *Spanish* in all necessary documents. According to researchers in the Vargas Project, *"almost all male heads of household"* were considered to be *español* in the caste system rankings of that point in history. Additionally, the communities from which they came also acknowledged them to be ranked *Spanish,* as were their wives and children. Thus it was reported to the Viceroy: *"All, it seems, are Spanish."*

In New Mexico these Spanish families tended to intermarry. *"Equally remarkable,"* upon marrying, the bride and groom *"could provide the names of both parents"* for marriage records. Further, the rate of illegitimate births in this group was very low, in contrast to the rates in New Spain and the mother country itself. [The El Paso people and the new recruits are the progenitors of New Mexico's present Hispano population. That means their ancestors arrived during the Oñate or Vargas colonizations.]

Following is a listing of individuals and/or groups who returned or came to New Mexico after the Pueblo Revolt. As indicated, all didn't arrive at the same time. [With regard to orthography, it must be kept in mind that names may and usually do have variant spellings. For example, *"Barela"* and *"Varela"* are the same name. It should also be pointed out that carrying the mother's surname, generally written after the father's surname, is an Hispanic tradition, as in *"López Castillo."* Finally, an "M" abbreviates *María*, a "J" for *José*]:

A:

Abalos: Antonio;

Abrego: Francisco; Francisca; Acosta: María;

Aguila: Miguel Gerónimo;

Aguilar: (Capt.) Alonso;

Aguilera: Pedro, M. Luisa;

Agular: J. Benito Isari; Antonio Isari;

Aguliar: Miguel Gerónimo;

Alamais: Manuela Antonia;

Alatia: María;

Alcalá: J. de Atienza;

Alemán: M. de la Cruz;

Almazán: Ana;

Anaya: Antonio de; Ana de; Juana; Francisco de Anaya; J. Salvador de Anaya; M. Josepha de;

Anaya: Ynes; (Capt.) Francisco;

Altamirino: Felipa Lechuga; Juan Tafoya; Nicolasa; Luis; Ancizo: Juana; Angel: Miguel;

Ángeles: Catalina de los; Antonio: Juan;

Anzures: Bartolomé; Gabriel, Juana; Teresa;

Apodaca: Cristóbal; Francisco; J. Gonzáles;

Aragón: Juan de Pedrasa; Antonio; Catalina Varela; Cristóbal; Félix; Francisco; Ignacio; Josefa Gonzáles; Juan; Juan Antonio; Juana; María;

Aranda: Mateo; Archuleta: Juan; Juana; Pablo; Pasquala; Juan; Andrés; Leonora; Juan; Cristóbal;

Aretia: (Capt.) Francisco;

Argüello: Juana;

Aris: Phelipa; Diego; J. Mateo; Joseph; Juana; Martín; Armijo: Antonio;

Arratia: Antonia; Juan Antonio; Mathais; Phelipa;

Arroyo: Diego; Arteaga: Felipe; M. López, Miguel;

Arvizu: Felipe; Tomás;

53

Aspeltia: Inés;
Atencia: Calstano; Francisco; Ignacio; Juan; María;
Atienza: José; Juan;
Avalos: Antonio; Juana; Pedro; Avila: María; Pedro Ayala: Diego Márquez;
 Antonio; Miguel;
Azate: Juan;

B:
Baca: Cristóbal; Felipe; Ignacio; Lenora; Manuel,
Bachiniva;
Balanegra: Simón;
Barba: Domingo Martín;
Barbosa: Simón;
Bejarano: Tomás;
Belásquez: Miguel;
Bernal: Francisco;
Betanzos: Andrés; Diego;
Brito: Agustín; Francisco; Joseph; Juan León;
Brixida: María;
Brusales: Juan;
Bustillos;
Busto: Juan de la Paz;

C:
Cabrera: Josefa; M. de Medina;
Cáceres: (Sgt.) Juan Ríos;
Caldana: Mateo; Camarillo: Diego;
Candelaria: Blas de la; Feliciano de la;
Carabajal: María;
Caras: Juana de Aras;
Cárdenas: Petronia;
Careres: Juan Ruiz;
Carrera: Tomás Gutiérrez de la;
Carrillo: M. Nicolasa;
Cásares: Juan Ruiz;
Casitias: Joseph;
Castillo: Isabel López del; José Cortez; Lucía del; (Sgt. Mayor) Diego del;
 Pedro López del; Castro: María; María Rodarte de; Cervantes: Juan
 Manuel Martínez; Manuel; María Zuniga y; Chávez: (Capt.) Fernando
 Durán y; Joseph Durán y; María; Pedro Durán y; Christina: Juana;
 Cisneros: María;

54

Coca: Miguel de la Vega y;
Concepción: Pascuala de la; San Juan de: María de la;
Contrertas: Joseph; Cordero: Juan Ruiz;
Córdoba: Antonio Coronanda: María;
Cortés: Juan;
Cortez: José;
Cortinas: Pedro;
Crisostomo: Juana;
Cruz: Tomás de la; Ana de la; Cecilia de la; María de la; Miguel de la;
Cruzate: (Capt. Gen.) Domingo Jironza Petriz de;
Cuellar: Cristóbal;
Cueva: Petronila de la;
Cuitar: Alonso Rodríguez de la;

D:
Dios: Juan de;
Dominíguez: Antonio; Francisco; José; Juan; Juana; Petrona; Petrolina;
    Joseph; Antonia; Durán: Antonia; Antonia Ursala; Antonio; Bartolomé;
    Catalina; Cristóbal; Diego; Francisco; Felipe; Josepha; Juana; Lázaro;
    Luis; María; Miguel; Salvador; Ysabel;

55

E:
Encarnación: María de la;
Escalante: Antonio Gonzáles;
Esperaza: Catallina Montoya;
Esparza: María;
Espindola: Catalina; Francisco;
Espinosa: Nicolás;
Esquibel: Juan Antonio; Esteban: Juan;
Estrada: Juan;

F:
Farfán: Fray Francisco;
Félix: Antonio;
Fernández: Diego Manuel de la Santísima Trinidad de;
Florida: Geronima Días;
Fontes: Cristóbal; Francisco; Josepha;
Foranco: Ygnacio de Santa María;
Fragua: Pedro;
Francisco: Matías; Fresque, Ambrosio;
Fresqui: Mariana;

G:

Gaitán: Isabel; Joseph;

Gallegos: Joseph;

Gamboa: Antonio; Ramírez; Manuel; Miguel; Juan; Phelipa;

Garas: Juana;

García: Ana María; Alonso; (Ensign) Alonso; Antonia; Antonio; Casilda; Cristóbal;

Diego; Elvira; Esteban López de; Felipe; Francisca; Francisco Jurado de; Ignacio López de; Juan; Juan de Noriega; Juan Esteban López de: Juan Jurado; Juana; Lucía; Luis; María; María Francisca; Miguel; Nicolás; Ramón; Theoria; Vicente;

Geuterero: Juana;

Gilteme: Joseph;

Girón: Rafaél Tellez;

Godines: Antonio; M. Luisa de Villaviecencio y; M. Luisa;

Godo: (Sgt. Mayor) Juan Lucero;

Godoy: Juan de Dios; Juan Lucero; María Luzero; Francisco Luzero; Nicolás Lucero;

Gómez: Antonio; Catalina; Diego; Domingo; Francisco; Josepha; Juan; Laureano; Manuel; Marcial; Margarita; M. de la Rosa; María; Thomana; Ursala;

Góngora: Cristóbal; Francisca; Gregoria; Juan de; Juana de; Juan Joseph; M. Gertrudis;

Gonzáles: Andrés; Antonia Blas; Catalina; Cristóbal; Damiana; Diego; María; Estefana; Francisco; Francisco de la Rosa; José; Josepha; Juana; Juan; Melchora de Los Reyes; Pedro; Petronia; (Councilman) Sebastián; Sevastián; Ysabel; Granillo: Domingo; Josepha; Juan; Luis; María; (Sgt. Mayor) Luis; Gregoria: Antonia; Juan;

Greimaldos: Diego Sánchez;

Griego: Ana Martín; (Ensign) Blas; Agustín; Catalina; Francisco; Juan; Lenor; María;

Grola (Gurule): Santiago;

Guadalajara: Jacinta;

Guatamala: Juana;

Guebara: Pedro;

Guerrero: Felipa,

Guerro: Juana;

Guevara: Juan de Fernández de Atienza Ladrón de; Miguel Ladrón de;

Guido: Juan;

Gutiérrez: Ana; Antonia; Juan Rogue (Roque); Miguel; Phelipe; Rogue;

H:

Heras: María de las;

Hernández: Francisco; Gertrudis;

Herrera: Antonio; Domingo; Gertrudis de la Candelaria; Josepha; Juan; Juana; Luisa; M. Tapia; Miguel; Sebastián; Ynes;

Hidalgo: (Ensign) Diego; Pedro;

Hinojos: Diego; Fernando; Josepha; Nicolás Ruiz;

Hita: Tomás;

Holguín: Cristóbal; (Capt.) Salvador; Juan; Juan López; Tomás;

Hurtado: Andrés; Catalina; Diego; Juan Páez; María; Mariana;

I:

Iñigo: Francisca Sánchez y; Jacinto Sánchez de; Pedro Sánchez;

Isasi: Antonio de Aguilera;

J:

Jaramillo: Cristóbal Varela; Lucía; Lucía Varela; Juan Varela; María; Yumar Varela;

Jirón: Diego; Isabel; Joseph Telles; Nicolás; Tomás;

Jorge: Antonio;

Jurado: J. García; Francisco;   57

L:

Lara: Ana Morena de;

Larea: Isabela;

Layba: Pedro; Juana;

Lechuga: Pedro;

León: Cristóbal;

Leyba: Francisco; Juana;

Linares: Miguel;

Lobato: Bartolomé;

López: (Ensign) Pedro; Angelo; (Capt.) Francisco; Carlos; Cristóbal; Francisco; Jacinto; José; Joseph; María; Nicolás; Pedro; (Sgt. Mayor) Diego;

Lorenzo: Francisco;

Losada: Juan Cristóbal; Lucía Varela; María Varela; Magdalena Varela; Pedro Varela;

Lucero: Antonio; Catalina; Francisco; Juan de Dios; Nicolás; (Sgt. Mayor) Diego;

Luis: (Capt.) Juan;

Luján: Agustín; (Capt.) Juan Luis; Cristóbal; Diego; Domingo; Isabel;

Josefa Juana; Juan; Matis (Matías?); Miguel; Pedro;

Luna: (Capt.) Diego; Diego; Juan;

Lusana: Clara,

Luxan: Agustine; Francisco; Luis, María;

M:

Machuca: Juan de Vargas;

Madrid: Francisco; (Capt.) Juan; Jacinto; José; Joseph; Juan, Juana; Lorenzo; Pedro; Rogue; (Sgt. Mayor) Lorenzo;

Maes: Luis;

Maese: Alonso; Alonso López; Luis; Miguel;

Magdalena: María;

Mandragón: Sebastián Monroy de;

Mantaño: José;

Manzanares: Ana de Sandoval y; Juan Mateo Sadoval y; María Sandoval; Sevastiana de Sandoval y; Marcelino; Cristóbal;

Marcos: Lucas;

Marín: Francisco;

Márquez: (Capt.) Antonio; Bernabé; Diego; Francisco; Juan; Juana Jaramillo y Zamora; Pedro;

Martín: (Ensign) Pedro; Antonio; Apoliar; Cristóbal; Diego; Domingo; Francisco; Hernando; Juan; Juana; Lucía; Luis; María; Pasquala; Pedro; Sevastián;

Martínez: Gerónimo; Juan de Dios Sandoval;

Mascareñas: J. Bernardo;

Mederos: (Capt.) Pedro López;

Medina: Alonso; Juan; Micaela; Manuela;

Méndez: Thomas;

Mendoza: Antonia; Antonio Dominíguez de; Francisco Dominíguez de; Juan Domingo; María; Tomé Dominíguez;

Mestas: Tomás;

Miguel: José;

Miranda; Miguel;

Mizquia: Lázaro;

Molina: Sebastián; Simón;

Montalvo: Rogue;

Montaño: Antonio; Catalina , Lucas; María;

Montero: Pedro;

Montesuma: Ysabel Caso;

Montiel: José;

Montoya: Ana María Griego; Antonio; Diego; Felipe; Francisca; Josepha;

María; Onafre; Phelipe;
Mora: Francisco de la; María;
Moraga: Ana; Antonia; Felipe; Lázaro; María;
Morales: Francisca;
Moreles: Juan;
Morán: Agueda; Miguel;
Moriello: Cristóbal;
Moya: Antonio;
Munier: Pedro;

N:
Naranjo: Pasqual;
Negrette: Manuela; José Jaramillo; Mateo;
Nevares: (Capt.) Joseph; José;
Nicolás: María de San;
Nieto: Cristóbal;
Noriega: Juan García de; Juana García de;
Nuñez: José;

O:
Ocanto: María;
Ochoa: Juan;
Ojeda: Antonio; Juana;
Olivas: Isabel; Juan de la Cruz y;
Olives: Juan Bautista;
Ontiveros: Francisco;
Órgano: Magdalena;
Orozco: Mariana Salas;
Ortega: Andrés; Dionisio; Josepha; María; Nicolás; Nicolás de; Pablo;
    Simón; Tiburcio;
Ortíz: Juana; María; Nicolás de; Nicolasa; Sebastiana;
Osuna: María;
Oton: Nicolás; Margarita;

P:
Pacheco: Acencio; Juan; Silvestre; Padilla: Joseph de; Páez: Agustine;
Palocios (Palacios): María de Encarnación; María de;
Palomino: Tomás; Papigochu;
Parades: Ganzalo de;
Parra: Gregorio Cobos de la; Pasqual Covos de la; Paz: Juan de la;
    Manuela;

59

Pedraza: Miguel; Francisco Romero;
Pedroza: Lázaro de Artiaga y;
Pelaez: Jacinto;
Peralta: Juan Bautista Anzaldo de;
Perca: Agustine; Antonia Varela; Isabel; Juan; Juana; Phelipe;
Porras: Francisco; Posada: (Capt.) Pedro Romero;

Q:
Quebara: Pedro;
Quintana: Miguel;
Quiros: Diego Aris de; José; Juana;

R:
Ramiréz: Gregorio; Nicolás; Petrona;
Ramos: Marcos; Miguel; Juan;
Reina: Juan;
Reinoso: Ana;
Rey: Nicolás Rodríguez;
Reyes: Agustine de los; Inés de los; María de los; Sebastián de los;
Ribera: Ana; Juan; Salvador Matías;
Rincón: Antonio Francisco;
Río: Alonso del; (Capt.) Alonso del; (Capt.) Juan del;
Ríos: Juana de los;
Riva: Miguel García de;
Rivera: Francisco; Josefa; Teresa;
Robledo: Ana María; Bartolomé Gómez; Francisco Gómez;
Rodon: Francisco Palamino;
Rodríguez: Agustín; Alonso; Francisca; José; Juan Severino; Manuel;
    Nicolás; Sebastián;
Rojas: Phelipa Rica de;
Romero: Baltazar; Bartolomé; Catalina; Diego; Felipe; Francisca;
    Francisco; Juan; Juan Antonio Juan Francisco; María; Phelipe; Salbador;
    Salvador;
Rosa: Antonia de la; María de la;
Roxas: Josepha Rico de; Ysabel Rico de;
Rueda: Juana;
Ruiz: Gregoria; Elena;

S:
Salas: Sebastián;
Salazar: Agustine; Baltazar Romero; Miguel; Francisca Ramiréz; Francisco;

Isabela; Lucía; María; Pedro; Martín Serrano;
Samano: María; San Juan de Concepción;
San Nicolás: María;
Sánchez: Felipe; Juan; José; Pedro;
Sandoval: Phelipa; Tomás de Herrera y;
Santiago: Francisco; José; Julián;
Santos: Juan de los;
Sayagoa: Antonia;
Sedana: Antonia; Josefa;
Sedillo: Felipa Rico de Rojas; Joachin Rico de Roxas; Juan Rico de Rixas;
   María de Nava; Pedro; Pedro de;
Senorga: María Luisa de;
Serna: Antonia de la; Cristóbal de la; Felipa de la;
Serrano: Fernando Martín; Sevastián Martín;
Sevillana: Gertrudis;
Sierra: Nicolás;
Silva: Antonia;
Sisneros: Antonio
Solís (Ensign);
Sonora;
Soria: Felipe;
Soto: Diego; Pasquala;
Sotomayor: María;
Suazo: Juan;
Susana: Clara,

T:
Tapia: Ana; Angela; Cristóbal; Lusía; María;
Tenorio: Miguel; Todos Santos San Bartolomé;
Torreón: Valle de;
Torres: Cristóbal: Francisco; Juana;
Toscano: Juan;
Trinadad: María;
Trujillo: Cristóbal; Cristóbal de (Elder); Cristóbal de (Younger); Damián;
   Diego; Bernadina de Salas y; Estafana; Gertrudis; Gregoria; Joseph
   Joaquín; Juan; Nicolás; Pasqual;

U:
Ulibarrí: Gertrudis Bautista de;

V:
Vaca: (Sgt. Mayor) Ygnacio;
Valdés: J. Luis;
Valencia: Francisco, Juan; Juana; Juana de;
Valenzuela: Antonia;
Valle: José del;
Vallejo: Manuel;
Vendura: Francisco;
Varela: Cristoval; Diego; Teresa; Francisco; José; Petrona; Polonia; Rogue;
Vargas: Diego de; Eusebio; Manuel; Vicente;
Vega; Francisca de la; Juana de la; María de la; Miguel de la;
Velasco: Cristóbal; (Capt.) Cristóbal de; Francisca; José; Micaela; Miguel
    García;
Velásquez: José;
Vera: Ana Jorge; Antonio; Isabel Jorge de; Melchor de; Vigil: Francisco
    Montes;
Villapando: Carlos; Juan;
Villasur: Pedro;

X:
Xaramillo: Pedro Varela; Xavier: (Capt.) Francisco;
Ximénez: Phelipa;
Xirón: (Capt.) Joseph Telles; Rafaél Telles;

Y:
Yñigo (Iñigo): Jacinto Sánchez; Pedro Sánchez; Ysabel: Bernardina;

Z:
Zambrano: Josepha; Zamora: Juan; María de Mora
Zarate: Miguel;
Zepidia: María de;
Zevin: Diego.

The Vargas colonizing expedition started up on October 4, 1693. It was late in the year for such an enterprise but that couldn't be helped. Besides, Santa Fe wasn't the other side of the world.

The weather turned cold very suddenly but the worst news was that the Pueblo Indians had experienced a change of heart and would no longer welcome the Christian colony. It was rumored they would fight to prevent the Christians from resettling the area.

In November when Vargas got to the area of present day Albuquerque he was warned by Juan de Ye that Picurís, Taos, Acoma, Jémez, etc., warriors, including some Apache and Navajo, were ready to fight Christian entry into Santa Fe. Vargas prepared his men for battle but at the same time he parleyed with Indian leaders, who decided not to fight after all. By December 16 the Christians made it to Santa Fe without having to combat insurgents but snow was coming down and it was now bitterly cold.

Santa Fe had been turned into an Indian village and its occupants refused to give it up. By Christmas Eve some 22 infants had died from exposure. Juan de Ye once more informed Vargas that warriors were coming to help the Indian defenders of Santa Fe. Vargas tried to resolve the impasse through diplomacy, promising that all Indians would remain free if they abandoned the city, that they would be killed if they fought. The Indians said they would fight to the death. The Captain General ordered the attack and after a fierce day of house-to-house battles and a final strike at dawn the next day, Christians once more possessed the City of the Holy Faith. Seventy warriors were executed and some 400 others were sentenced to ten years of servitude.

Santa Fe was now resettled but even basic survival would be no simple feat and there was the continued threat of attack from other Indians.

In January of 1694 Pecos leader Juan de Ye informs Vargas that a large force of hostile Indians are coming to attack Pecos Pueblo because of the help they have given the Christians. Vargas sends second-in-command Roque de Madrid with 30 professional soldiers to defend the village. He also states that if necessary, Vargas himself will bring more soldiers if called upon. The hostiles see that Pecos Pueblo is well defended so the attack doesn't take place. Juan de Ye and his Pecos people are now steadfast allies of Vargas and his colony.

Military expeditions are sent against San Ildefonso Pueblo, without success, but the Christians, aided by Pueblo auxiliaries led by Bartolomé de Ojeda, win at Santo Domingo and Cochití.

In time more settlers arrived. Father Francisco Farfán and Capt. Cristóbal de Velasco brought the following pioneers, known as the *Españoles Mexicanos* (Spanish-Mexicans) from the City and valley of Mexico, to New Mexico in the spring of 1694 [names may have variant spellings as indicated above]:

A:
Aguila, Miguel Gerónimo del (with spouse Gerónima Días Florida, one child);
Aguilera, Pedro de (with spouse Juana de Torres, four children);
Aguilera Isasi, Antonio (with spouse Gertrudis Hernández, one child);

Anzures, Gabriel (with spouse Felipa Lechuga de Altamirino, one or two children);

Aragón, Ignacio (with spouse Sebastiana Ortiz, three children);

Atienza, Juan (widower, two children);

Atienza, José (with spouse Estafana de Trujillo and her two brothers, Damián and Joseph Joaquín Trujillo);

Atienza Alcalá, José (with spouse Gertrudis Sevillana);

B:

Betanzos, Andrés (widower, with two sons);

Betanzos, Diego (with spouse María Luisa de Senorga);

Busto, Juan de La Paz (with spouse Manuela Antonia de Alamias, two children);

C:

Cárdenas, Andre (with spouse Juana de Avalos, two children);

Castellanos, José (with spouse Manuela de Paz and their five children);

Cervantes, Manuel de (with spouse Francisca Rodríguez);

Cortés, Juan (with spouse Juana de Aras [Caras?] with one to three children);

Cortés del Castillo, José (with spouse María de Carbajal, two children);

D:

Dios, Juan de (with spouse and son);

E:

Esquibel, Juan Antonio (with spouse María de San Nicolás, two children);

F:

Fernández de Atienza Ladrón de Guevara (with spouse Teresa de Rivera, one child);

G:

Gamboa, Juan (with spouse María de Zepidia, three children);

Gamboa, Manuel (with spouse Ysabel Caso Montesuma);

Gamboa, Miguel (with spouse);

García Jurado, José (with spouse Josepha, de Herrera, and their two sons);

García de Riva, Miguel (with spouse Micaela Velasco and their five children);

Godines, Antonio (widower, with daughter);

Góngora, Cristóbal (with spouse Inés de Aspeitia);

Góngora, Juan (with spouse Petronila de la Cueva, five children);

H:
Herrera y Sandoval, Tomás de (with spouse Pascuala de la Concepción, two children);

J:
Jaramillo Negrete, José (with spouse María Sotomayor, three children);
Jirón, Diego (with spouse María de Mendoza, two children);
Jirón, Nicolás (with spouse Josefa Sedano);
Jirón, Tomás (with spouse Josefa Gonzáles de Aragón, two children);

L:
Ladrón de Guevara, Miguel (with spouse Felipa Guerrero, one child);
Leyba, Francisco;
Lorenzo, Francisco (with spouse and one child);
Luján, Juan (with spouse Petrona Ramiréz, one child);

M:
Marcelino, Cristóbal (with spouse Juana de Góngora);
Márquez de Ayala, Diego (with spouse María de Palacios, two children);
Martínez de Cervantes, Juan Manuel (with spouse Catalina de los Ángeles and a maid Cecilia de la Cruz;
Mascareñas, José Bernardo (with spouse María de Acosta, two children);
Medina, Juan (with spouse Juana Jaramillo y Zamora Márquez);
Medina, Juan de (with spouse Antonia Sedana, a sister of Josefa Sedana above, married to Nicolás Jirón);
Molina, Simón (with spouse Micaela de Medina);
Moya, Antonio (with spouse Francisca Morales);

N:
Nuñez, José (with spouse Gertrudis de la Candelaria Herrera);

O:
Ortiz, Nicolás (with spouse María Coronada, six children);

P:
Palomino, Tomás (with spouse Gertrudis Bautista de Ulibarrí, two children);
Porras, Francisco de (with spouse Damiana Gonzáles, one child);

65

Q:

Quintana, Miguel (with spouse Gertrudis de Trujillo, sister of Estafana Trujillo above);

R:

Rodríguez, José (with spouse María de Sarnano, three children);

Rodríguez, Manuel (with spouse María de la Encarnación Palacios, one child);

Rincón, Antonio Francisco (with spouse Antonia de Valenzuela, three children);

Romero, Juan Francisco (with spouse María de Avila);

Rosa Gonzáles, Francisco de la (with spouse Antonia de la Serna);

Ruiz Cordero, Juan (with spouse María Nicolassa. Carrillo);

S:

Salas, Sebastián (with spouse María García);

Sánchez de Hita, Tomás Fulano (with spouse Antonia Gutiérrez, one child; Tomás died in Zacatecas and Antonia continued to NM where she married Juan de Archibeque in 1697);

Sánchez, José (with spouse Josefa Gómez de Rivera, with father in law José Cortez);

Sayago, Antonio (with spouse María de Mora Zamora, two children);

Silva, Antonio (with spouse Gregoria Ruiz, one child);

T:

Trujillo, Nicolás (with spouse María Luisa de Aguilera, four children; returned to Mexico City in 1705);

V:

Valdés, José Luis (with spouse María de Medina Cabrera, two children);

Valle, José del (with spouse Ana de Ribera, with adopted child Bernardino Sena);

Vallejo, Manuel (widower, one child);

Velasco, Francisca (widow, with nephew Miguel García Velasco and niece Manuela);

Velasco, José (with spouse María de Tapia Herrera, one child);

Vega y Coca, Manuel de la (spouse Manuela Medina and mother in law Josefa de Cabrera).

[Three Frenchmen had been captured before the Pueblo Revolt and now returned to NM with stripes on their faces: Pedro Munier, Santiago Grola, and Juan de Archibeque.]

In June of 1694 Vargas leads an expedition up north. Taos is found deserted but Taos leader Francisco Pacheco appears unexpectedly with heavily armed warriors, which include Apaches. Juan de Ye translates for Vargas. No agreement is reached but Pacheco invites his friend Juan de Ye to spend the night in the Taos camp for further discussion. Because of the friendship between the two, the Pecos leader accepts.

The following morning no one shows up to negotiate. Vargas sends hurried messages that Juan de Ye must be returned immediately or Taos Pueblo will be attacked. There is no response so Vargas' men break into the pueblo but Juan de Ye is nowhere to be found. Vargas realizes that the duplicitous Taos have murdered his friend and ally. Pueblo stores of corn are confiscated and delivered to the colonists.

In July Vargas leads a campaign to the west, attacking Jémez, Acoma, the Hopi, and some Apache bands, all successful. The final campaign is now against Tesuque Pueblo and when that is successful the Reconquest is complete.

In May of 1695 Capt. Juan Páez Hurtado arrives in Santa Fe with more livestock and some 45 new families. The new colonists are from the Zacatecas – Sombrerete area of Mexico and include:

67

Aranda, Mateo (with Teresa de la Cruz and María Rodríguez);

Arellano, Cristóbal (with his sister and niece);

Armijo, Antonio (with spouse Manuela Negrete and Antonio's brother Marcos);

Camarillo, Diego (with spouse Antonia García);

Cortinas, Pedro (with spouse María Ortiz and a son);

Crisóstomo, Juana (with Toribio Nicolás and Juana Nicolasa);

Durán, Catalina (widow with three children);

Espinosa, Nicolás (with a sister and brother);

Félix, Antonio (with spouse Francisca Valencia, one son and two nephews);

López, José (with spouse María Osuna, one daughter);

Marcos, Lucas (with Juana de Guadalupe and Juan Nicolás);

Gómez, Laureano (with spouse Josefa Cruz and a nephew);

González, Francisco (with two cousins, Baltazar Rodarte and Terese de Jesús Rodarte);

Guerro, Juana (with a son and daughter);

Guido, Juan (with spouse Isabel de los Reyes Ribera and a son);

Hernández, Francisco (with spouse Juana García and one son);

Lobato, Bartolomé (with spouse Luisana Negrete and one son);

López, Angela (and her two brothers Juan and Antonio Ortiz);

Martínez, Jerónimo (with spouse Antonia de la Rosa and a daughter);

Méndez, Tomás (with spouse María de la Cruz and one daughter);

Montalve, Roque Pantoja (with two other people, Miguel Gutiérrez and his sister Natiana);

Montes Vigil, Francisco (with spouse María Jiménez Armijo);

Montes Vigil, Juan;

Morillo, Cristóbal (with Sebastián Canseco and María Gutiérrez);

Miranda, Miguel (with a daughter and son);

Negrete, Mateo (with spouse Simona Bejar and one daughter);

Olivas, Isabel (with daughter and her brother José Rodríguez);

Olives, Juan Bautista (with spouse Magdalena Juárez and daughter);

Quiros, José (with a daughter and a nephew);

Quiros, Juana (with a son and nephew);

Ramos, Marcos (with spouse Isabela Larea);

Ramos, Miguel (with sister Antonia and a servant Josefa de la Rosa);

Reina, Juan (with spouse María Encarnación and a nephew);

Reinoso, Ana (with daughter and son);

Reyes, Inés de los (with a daughter and son);

Reyes, María de los (with daughter María Canseco and nephew Nicolás Ararmujes);

Ribera, Salvador Matías (with spouse Juana Rosa and one son);

Rodríguez, Agustín (with spouse Nicolasa Ortiz);

Rodríguez, Sebastiana (widow with three children);

Romero, Juan Antonio (with two nieces and one nephew);

San Nicolás, María de (with a son and daughter);

Santos, Juan de los (with spouse Josefa Cristina Durán and a nephew);

Soria, Felipe (with spouse María Castro and one son);

Tenorio, Miguel (with a daughter and Cristóbal Rodríguez);

Trinadad, María de la (widow with two sons);

Zarate, Miguel (with spouse María de la Rosa and a son).

[It has been observed that New Mexicans of the 17th and 18th centuries became "one big family" through intermarriage. Common greetings often used the words *"primo/prima"* (cousin) when saying hello.]

It was thought in January of 1695 that New Mexico was finally at peace but in June of 1696 the Taos, Picurís, Cochití, Santo Domingo, Jémez, and the Tewa pueblos rise in rebellion, killing some 21 soldier-settlers as well as 5 missionaries. The pueblos of Pecos, Tesuque, San Felipe, Santa Ana, and Zía remain loyal and refuse to join the uprising.

Bartolomé de Ojeda from Picurís writes to Roque de Madrid that warriors from Hopi, Zuñi, Acoma, possibly with Ute confederates, are planning to wipe out the Christian colony once and for all. Lucas Naranjo of Cochití is leading the rebels.

Vargas advises all settlers to withdraw to fortified communities. With soldiers, colonists, and Pueblo auxiliaries, he battles the Jémez, Acoma, and Zuñi warriors, successfully, and food supplies are confiscated. Lucas Naranjo is killed at the battle of El Embudo. The northern campaign is reopened, fighting is done when necessary, but rebel food supplies are the real targets, the lack of which in the end force rebel forces to surrender.

By December of 1695 there is finally established a permanent peace in New Mexico. Governor Diego de Vargas has been true to his promise: he has reestablished the Christian colony in New Mexico and despite some Pueblos rejecting peace and openly opting for war, the Pueblo people have not been exterminated.

Documentation for PART VI – DIEGO de VARGAS

1. Kessell, John L., and Hendricks, Rick, and Dodge, Meredith D. (eds.) *To the Royal Crown Restored.* Albuquerque: University of New Mexico Press, 1995, pp. 9-21. This is "A Volume in the Journals of don Diego de Vargas" produced by the Vargas Project at the University of New Mexico. These volumes are a monumental contribution to New Mexico, Southwest, and American historiography. The shorter classic work on Vargas and the recolonization is *Crusaders of the Río Grande: The Story of Don Diego de Vargas and the Reconquest and Refounding of New Mexico* by J. Manuel Espinosa, published in 1942.

Part VII
Alliance

⌒

B
Y 1703 THE HEROIC DIEGO DE VARGAS, NOW WITH THE
prestigious title of *Marqués de la Nava Braziñas,* was once more
Governor of New Mexico. He needed men to defend the province so
he tapped available Pueblo sources. This might not appear spectacular but
Vargas initiated a new era when the governor included tough Pueblo Indian
fighters in the 1704 expedition against the Faraón Apache raiders.

Captain Félix Martínez of the presidio supplied 50 soldiers while the
Tewas, Keres, and Pecos pueblos were asked to select warriors for the expedition. Pueblos willing to fight came from Pecos, San Felipe, Santo Domingo,
Cochití, Nambé, Tesuque, San Ildefonso, Santa Clara, San Juan, Jémez, Zía,
and Santa Ana, comprising some 120 tough Pueblo warriors.

Joseph Naranjo and thirty Amerindians were sent ahead to scout the
terrain leading to the Sandía Mountains in an effort to locate the hostiles.
A skirmish took place but on April 2 Vargas was stricken with a fatal illness
and the expedition comes to an abrupt halt. Vargas is taken to the home of
Fernando Durán y Chaves in Bernalillo. Diego de Vargas, paladin of New
Mexico and New Spain, dies on April 8, 1704.

Governor Vargas had begun an effective Spanish policy (in fact, started
by Cortés in Mexico): Hispanic and Pueblo people were united against the
menace of hostile tribes like the Apache, Comanche, Utes, and some bands
of Navajo. Together the Spanish and Pueblos might survive the onslaught,
despite being seriously outnumbered by the *indios bárbaros,* nomadic tribes.
Hostiles would therefore have to face professional soldiers, armed settlers,
with mounted and armed Pueblo warriors.

The Pueblo people supplied courageous warriors, interpreters who
knew various Amerindian languages, foodstuffs and other necessary supplies. More important in the long run, Amerindians from various groups
saw the Pueblos allied with Spanish New Mexicans. They saw the fruits of
Hispanicization among native people and they must have wondered what

might happen to them if they walked the white path of peace.

Government and Church officials took care to preserve the Pueblo people. In 1706 Governor Cuervo y Valdés sent Juan de Ulibarrí to recover the Picurís who had fled to the Apaches after the revolt of 1696. The Picurís had sought freedom from Spanish domination but instead they had been enslaved by their former allies living in the area of the Cuartelejo Apaches (what is now Pueblo, Colorado). Some 62 destitute Picurís were loaned horses and given supplies for the return to their native village. [1]

The Ulibarrí freedom expedition is considered the highlight of Cuervo's administration and an excellent example of emerging Hispanic-Pueblo unity. Further, the hostile tribes now had a first-hand example that former enemies would not be mistreated or exterminated.

The year 1706 is also important for the introduction of the office called "Protector General of the Indians." [2] Not only were Pueblo Indians being acculturated to the dominant society, they now had a cabinet level officer to turn to when they felt they needed him.

As might be expected in human behavior, there were some disagreements over the years. Spanish authorities, secular and clerical, still would not condone Pueblo scalp dances. It was considered un-Christian to dance in celebration over human body parts, even those of enemies. Also, some Pueblos were thought to be trading with the nomadic, hostile tribes. Regardless, the Pueblo-Spanish alliance continued and census figures show that Pueblo population "...*seems to have increased.*"[3]

71

While it had been preliminary Spanish policy not to arm the Indians and to deny them horses, this was not true with Pueblo allies. They were permitted to acquire horses as well as firearms. Just like Spanish soldiers and militiamen, they were encouraged to wear leather jackets as a defense against enemy arrows. There was also some concern that Pueblos painting themselves for war might lead to being confused with painted enemy warriors.

In 1726 Brigadier Pedro de Rivera made an inspection of New Mexico. He recommended retention of the 80 soldiers of the Santa Fe presidio but he was not pleased with their involvement in commercial activities. He commented favorably on the Pueblo people, saying they were of better appearance than most Indians; that they dressed properly, they were hard workers, etc., that they all traveled on horseback. Their houses were attractive despite being constructed for defensive purposes. He was especially impressed with their willingness to combat their hostile enemies without submitting a bill to the Royal Treasury. He concluded their loyalty was beyond question and he thanked them for it.

In the 1730s there were still Apache raids but fewer than before. Perhaps the nomadic tribes were considering the Pueblo example of peaceful coexistence? Or perhaps potential hostiles were aware of immediate response to raids. All Spanish settlers and Pueblos were subject to an immediate call to go out on the campaign trail. All able bodied men were expected to serve for up to 15 days at a time when called upon to do so.

Comanches, an extremely large tribe of warrior people, starting coming into New Mexico in the early 1700s. They were so powerful they displaced the fierce Apaches from eastern New Mexico and took it over for themselves. (It can be observed that the province was surrounded by Utes to the north, Comanches to the east, Apaches to the south, and Navajos to the west.) Comanches fought with everyone, including Spaniards and Pueblos alike.

It has been written that without Hispanos the Pueblo people would never have been able to survive if the warlike tribes had desired to exterminate them. A.B. Thomas wrote in his *Forgotten Frontiers* that New Mexican Spaniards *"...came as saviors..."* for the Pueblo people. *"Against starvation the padre's prayer and Spanish grain supported them; barbarian inroads met the steel of Spanish courage. The unwritten record of this heroic defense of New Mexico is limned with Spanish blood that alone saved the distinctive Pueblo Southwest and dulled the edge of surrounding savagery..."*[4]

Governor Tomás Vélez Cachupín (1749-1754) was the only one able to pacify the Comanches. He followed Spanish policy: first he defeated them in battle (campaign of 1751) then invited them to live in peace, *like the Pueblos.* The warrior Comanches accepted and, in an unprecedented move, some of them took part in Spanish-Pueblo campaigns against Apaches. It appeared Pueblo warriors held themselves in check for they harbored deep-seated animosities toward Apaches, Comanches, and Utes. But they kept the peace promoted by Spanish civil and religious authorities.

The peace held while Vélez Cachupín was in office, fell apart when he left New Mexico, but was regained when he returned for his second term (1762-1767), then fell apart once more until Anza became governor.

Juan Bautista de Anza was already considered a native Hispanic hero of New Spain when he became governor of New Mexico (1778-1788). Raiders, especially Comanches, had the province on the brink of ruination.

Cuerno Verde (Green Horn) was a fearless Comanche leader considered *"the scourge of New Mexico."* He hated New Mexico because, it is said, his father was killed there. Anza understood he would have to defeat Cuerno Verde in all out battle in order to impress the other Comanche bands.

The governor put together a force of some 600 fighters that included Pueblos as well as some conciliated Jicarillas and Utes. The Indians numbered around 259 and were all too happy to fight Comanches. Just as important was that Spanish governmental leaders were actually achieving unity among formerly warring groups. (This was considered very progressive because friendly Indians weren't a threat to settled communities.)

Instead of taking the expedition through Taos, where spies would see them coming, Anza leads (1779) his force through Ojo Caliente (then to Poncha Pass, Ute Pass, and down into present Colorado Springs) and comes into the San Luis Valley from the north, totally surprising the Comanche encampment. But the warriors are away raiding in Taos. As they return with their spoils they find Anza's army waiting for them.

Cuerno Verde's men are virtually surrounded but the chief comes out alone, his horse curveting spiritedly in full view of his enemies. The Comanches hold no thoughts of surrender and there begins a bloody battle of no quarter. The hostile Comanches fight heroically to the last man, none being taken alive.

Spoils, which included a horse herd of more than 500 animals and so much baggage and goods that it couldn't be loaded on a hundred horses, are divided up and the expedition journeys back home. The Indians might not have been aware that they were being pulled to a more peaceful way of life but they did express their joy in being victorious against their Comanche enemies.

By 1785 there are Comanche bands that want peace with Governor Anza and Spanish and Pueblo New Mexico. Anza informs them that all bands and their rancherías (encampments; said to number more than 600) must make peace if they sincerely wish to stabilize the frontier for all people. It appears that most Comanches want peace with New Mexicans, Spanish and Pueblo alike.

73

The COMANCHE PEACE

In 1786 Chief Ecueracapa, also known as *Cota de Malla,* leads his people to Pecos Pueblo then is escorted to Santa Fe to sign a peace treaty with Governor Anza.

Chief Ecueracapa is received with honors and festivities due any Chief of State: a military escort, the entire town council in attendance, and the assembled crowd applauding at every turn.

Anza and Ecueracapa go into the *Casas Reales* (Palace of the Governors) where there is waiting a sullen delegation of *Utes,* who have always been attacked by Comanches. The very word *Comanche* is Ute for *enemy* or *wants to fight me all the time.* Anza suggests that now is the time for the two warrior groups to make peace. The Utes hesitate then say they will if Ecueracapa will. The Comanche chieftain declares his people will make peace with the Utes. One more vitally important step is taken toward stabilizing frontier New Mexico.

After three days of festivities and conferencing everyone adjourns to

Pecos Pueblo where the Comanche Peace is finalized. The treaty stipulates that Comanches may come to Santa Fe to trade. Trade fairs will be established at Pecos and rules will prevent Indians from getting cheated. Comanches will help fight hostile Apaches, etc. The Spanish governor would support any leader chosen by the various Comanche bands.

Spanish New Mexico was experiencing its greatest single event in frontier Hispano-Amerindian history. *The fearless Comanche warriors were actually making peace!*

Anza is in his element. He visits various Comanche camps and dines with them when invited. The Comanches crowd around him at every opportunity, embracing him, rubbing their faces against his as is the Comanche custom. For all time, among the warrior Comanches he would indeed be *The Great Captain.*

Even after Anza and Ecueracapa were gone from New Mexico, the peace forged at Pecos Pueblo stood unbroken for generations and is a testament to the historical Spanish policy of incorporating Native American groups into frontier society power structures, all begun (in what is now the USA) with the Hispano and Pueblo people of New Mexico.

New Mexico would prosper as Hispano and Pueblo men of commerce went out into the plains to trade. The age of the *cibolero* (buffalo lancer), *comanchero* (Pueblo and Hispano traders), and *mesteñero* (wild horse cowboy) was to go into full bloom because there was relative peace on the plains.

The Hispano-Pueblo alliance of New Mexico was and remains the most effective Euro-Amerindian cooperative venture in the history of what is now the USA. The Hispano-Comanche alliance is second only to that of the Pueblos. As indicated, when other Amerindian groups observed the Pueblos' success they were encouraged to make peace in order to live more fruitful, productive lives. When the Comanches followed their example it was a success that never again would be experienced in what is now the United States of America. Hispanic New Mexicans achieved what no one else ever did in the history of the USA.

These sterling events far surpassed the Pueblo Revolt and its atrocities. Perhaps it could be said that the massacre of 1680, which didn't cause the extermination of the Pueblo people, finally resulted in the Comanche Peace that enabled Spanish New Mexicans and Amerindian societies to live with each other in relative peace. As is often said, this time not in derogation: *Only in New Mexico.*

Documentation for PART VII – ALLIANCE

1. Jones, Oakah L. *Pueblo Warriors & Spanish Conquest.* Norman: University of Oklahoma Press, 1966, p. 76. This is perhaps the best study of Spanish-

Pueblo unity though the focus is more on the Pueblos.

2. Cutter, Charles R. *The Protector de Indios in Colonial New Mexico, 1659-1821.* Albuquerque: University of New Mexico Press, 1986. As Dr. Cutter says in the Foreword: *"Spain, unlike other colonial powers, wrestled mightily with moral and legal questions about the provision for justice in the colonies. The protector, who was appointed by the Spanish government, represented the legal rights and privileges of the Indians."*

3. *Pueblo Warriors & Spanish Conquest,* p. 85.

4. Thomas, Alfred Barnaby. *Forgotten Frontiers: A Study of the Spanish Indian Policy of Don Juan Bautista de Anza, Governor of New Mexico, 1777-1787.* Norman: University of Oklahoma Press, 1932, p. 84.

Part VIII
Review of the Literature
~

THE FOLLOWING ARE WORKS ON THE PUEBLO REVOLT THAT should be accessible to most interested readers. They are presented according to the dates of publication and could be said to represent what has been written on the Pueblo Revolt.

1970
Silverberg, Robert. *The Pueblo Revolt.* Lincoln: University of Nebraska Press, 1970.

After an introduction by Marc Simmons, Silverberg mentions the beginning of the Oñate colony and by page 3 the reader is told, *"For Spain it was a cruel harvest..."* of Spanish greed for gold, slavery and fanatical religion. The Amerindians in Spanish lands *"...were treated with chilling inhumanity."* Christianity was forced on the Indians and they became slaves of the ferocious Spanish empire. Indians who fought back were *"...slaughtered like beasts."* Indian leaders showing nobility and intelligence were automatically executed to avoid future problems. *"Terror...was routine...Spanish policy."* Native Indian groups couldn't survive the onslaught of *"...Spanish ferocity and diseases the Spaniards brought...the martyrdom of the Indians at the hands of Spain was one of history's darkest episodes."*

In Chapter 4 Silverberg writes that after the Acoma War all males over the age of twenty-five *"...were to have one foot chopped off..."* then sentenced to twenty years of *"...personal service, the dainty Spanish phrase that meant slavery."* He goes on to state that by 1629 a new Acoma church was being built, along with basic mission buildings. In the mission gardens one could find *"...orchards of fruit unfamiliar to the Pueblos...pears, peaches, figs, dates, pomegranates, olives, cherries, quinces, lemons, oranges, nectarines."*

The Pueblo people of New Mexico were forced to build churches and houses *"...for the invaders..."* They performed slave labor in the fields and protests were met with execution. This was endured until 1680 when *"...the placid, gentle Pueblo Indians rose up against their oppressors..."*

Silverberg takes up the actual Revolt causes in Chapter 6. He writes that in 1675 Governor Treviño had some 47 medicine men rounded up and imprisoned in Santa Fe. A San Juan medicine doctor from San Juan pueblo, Popé, was one of the healers whipped. Popé was perhaps 50 or 60 years old and he had fought Christianity all his life in favor of the kiva religion. *"Often he had clashed with the Spaniards..."* and the missionaries could not trust him so they had him punished numerous times. Popé and others planned the revolt, a holy war as well as one of vengeance. The message was clear: you are either with us or against us. When Nicolás Bua, Popé's son-in-law and governor of San Juan Pueblo, refuses to join the conspiracy, Popé has him murdered. This act sent out the message that no enemy was to be spared.

The uprising was to begin on August 13 but when the secret was discovered August 10 became the day of death and destruction. Silverberg writes that the 47 captives taken by Governor Otermín had stated *"...the Pueblo gods had decreed the death of every male Spaniard in New Mexico..."* With no other recourse left at their disposal, the Spanish people of New Mexico were forced out to El Paso where they lived for twelve years.

Popé was now the supreme governor of New Mexico. He lived in Santa Fe and took to wearing *"...a fantastic outfit of gaudy hued robes, and wearing a bull's horn on his forehead as a symbol of his authority."* He had some Indians enslaved because they had refused to join the rebellion. His reign became as burdensome as that of the Spaniards. He was soon replaced and it is said he died in 1688. 77

Diego de Vargas returned in 1692 and after more fighting, reestablished Spanish New Mexico.

Silverberg ends his book saying *"the white man"* had ruined the Pueblo people in a mere eighty years, *"...leaving them incapable of governing themselves...soured by tribal rivalry..."* He asks why it was necessary for Spaniards to come and take Indian land. He says that according to Indians, *"You came to steal our land because you wanted it...you came, and stole..."*

1995

Knaut, Andrew L. *The Pueblo Revolt of 1680: Conquest and Resistance in Seventeenth-Century New Mexico.* Norman: University of Oklahoma Press, 1995.

Dr. Knaut begins his work by stating that there are problems in studying the Amerindian past through archaeology as well as records left by *"Spanish missionaries, settlers, and colonial officials."* He asserts that *"collec-*

tive Pueblo memory" might have become clouded over the centuries. Also, documentary Spanish language evidence *"reflects all too faithfully the biases of Spanish observers..."*

Historian H.E. Bolton's works are described as paying scant attention to Amerindian issues and not being able to "Parkmanize" subject matter, as did Francis Parkman.

Dr. Knaut states his book is an attempt to study 17th century New Mexico by using Indians and the Pueblo Revolt of 1680 as a focal point. Among the main reasons for revolt were Spanish persecution of native practices, raids by hostile Apaches, along with famine and epidemic disease.

The purpose of the revolt was to kill all Spanish people in New Mexico. The initial slaughter was successful because no one was expecting the uprising. Survivors fled to Santa Fe in self-defense but finally the group holed up there had to leave for safety in El Paso. The refugees were able to witness some of the destruction that took place all over New Mexico north of Isleta Pueblo.

In Part I of Dr. Knaut's historical review he states *"Intimidation was the key to Spanish authority among the Pueblo Indians..."* Spaniards like Coronado followed a pattern of violence and brutality to suppress the Indians, who now considered Spanish people to be *"ragtag looters and murderers."* By the time of Oñate laws required a more Christian, humane policy but the Acoma revolt was put down brutally with *"all Acoma males over twenty-five years of age to have one foot cut off..."*

In Part II the reader is told *"...Juan de Oñate and his settlers in 1598 injected turmoil into Pueblo society..."* Established trading patterns with other Indians were also disrupted.

The Hispanic community was also hopelessly divided between governmental authorities, the Franciscans, and the Spanish settlers at large. Indians recognized the divisions and were puzzled.

Spanish demands for food and clothing were collected ruthlessly. Some men *"...took blankets away from the Indian women, leaving them naked and shivering with cold."*

The Pueblos had a long history of trading with the nomads of the Great Plains. While there were raids at times, trade *"was by far the most common form of interaction."* Spaniards disrupted the trade and *"...fueled animosity between the two groups."* Further, by introducing new grains, cattle, horses, metal tools, etc., Spaniards *"...added grounds for conflict..."* And of course, the Spanish could be blamed for bringing horses that facilitated raiding parties that were so injurious to the Pueblo people.

While Christianity was a path to some forms of security, various Franciscan missionaries were brutally martyred.

Some *mestizos* [half-bloods] became a part of Hispanic society while others gravitated toward the Pueblos. Some mestizos rose in Spanish society, *"...a rarity in an empire rigid in its caste-oriented prejudices."*

Relations between Church and State authorities were turbulent at best. This was so because they each wanted to control the Indians and use them for their own gain. Governors could arrest and prosecute whomever they targeted while the Franciscans could excommunicate and bring someone before the Inquisition. Settlers could support either, putting themselves at risk from the powers of the other side. Indians watched and waited.

Part III begins with the observation that the *"...mystique of Spanish omnipotence...fell into jeopardy."* Yet there would be an acculturation that dimmed distinctions from the European and Pueblo worlds through miscegenation. Despite these facts *"Pueblo society suffered from famine... diseases...labor and tribute demands of colonial overlords...hostilities from surrounding Athabaskans."*

It has been estimated that prior to the revolt there were some 2500 to 3000 Hispanics living in New Mexico.

Pueblo ways were becoming Hispanic ways. Oñate's vision *"...of Spanish domination through cultural separation and superiority..."* was dead. Hispanic faces were now looking like Indian faces because Hispanics mixed with the Pueblos though *"No quantitative data exist..."* but there was definitely a *"...scarcity of Spanish pure-bloods..."* In 1677 there arrived 43 new soldiers, 40 of them were convicts.

One of the reasons Hispanics accepted Pueblo practices was the scarcity of medicine on this frontier. There were no doctors so Franciscans generally were sought out for cures, if one was available. Many people turned to *"...indigenous folk medicine and curanderismo..."* which was a contribution of Pueblo culture. Further, *"...settlers also accepted and participated in ceremonial rites..."* with Apaches and Navajos. The Inquisition also recorded this type of documentation.

Chapter Eight begins with the information that *"...Franciscan and Spanish colonial rule...inflicted suffering to an unprecedented degree upon New Mexico's native inhabitants."* Pueblo population diminished noticeably due to *"European diseases,"* drought, famine, and a harsh *"...Spanish colonial system..."* though *"Documentary evidence...is scarce..."* except in *"...a few scattered references..."* Heavy demands for tribute *"...aggravated Pueblo suffering..."*

Francisco Xavier, Governor Treviño's secretary of government and war, targeted medicine men, especially *"...his unremitting persecution of one medicine man in particular,"* Po'pay from San Juan Pueblo, who *"...remains hidden in historical obscurity."* Po'pay worked in the utmost secrecy but he was able to weld together leaders from various pueblos in order to channel *"...more*

79

than eighty years of Pueblo fury..." New Mexico's Hispanic community would pay the bloody price, which would result in their ejection from the province for twelve years.

Po'pay had been thoroughly influenced by Spanish oppressors because now he demanded tribute like the Spaniards. In a short time Luis Tupatú from Picurís deposed him. By 1683 Tupatú sent an emissary to El Paso with an invitation for Hispanics to return to Santa Fe. Diego de Vargas would reestablish Spanish authority beginning in 1692. Dr. Knaut finishes by saying: *"Miscegenation continued to erase the genetic lines separating the land's native inhabitants from the newest set of colonists for the remainder of the colonial period...weaving the two peoples together into the complex tapestry that represents New Mexico's colonial heritage."*

2002
Preucel, Robert W. (ed.) *Archaeologies of the Pueblo Revolt: Identity, Meaning, and Renewal in the Pueblo World.* Albuquerque: University of New Mexico Press, 2002.

Titled *"The Holy War,"* the preface to this work was written by Herman Agoyo, a former governor of San Juan Pueblo *(Ohkay Owingeh).* Agoyo states that in 1976 he was basically unaware that 1980 would be the 300th anniversary of the *"Great Pueblo Revolt"* until someone from the Smithsonian Institution *"...alerted me."*

Agoyo believes Po'pay might have been a religious leader but very little is known about him, before or after the Revolt.

A couple of Coronado's and Zaldívar's *"...bloody episodes still live in Pueblo memory..."* In Tiguex, Coronado *"...evicted the Indians from their homes."* Zaldívar got revenge on the Acomas. Oñate was brutal when he sentenced *"...Acoma males, 25 years and older, to have one foot hacked off."* In 1998 Oñate was still controversial for the 400th anniversary of the founding of Hispanic New Mexico.

In 1997 Senator Manny Aragon sponsored Senate Bill 404 that created a Statuary Hall Commission which was to raise funds for a statue of Popé to be enshrined in Statuary Hall, while *"...adversaries whose outlandish claims against Pope's heroic efforts..."* went unheeded. For the Pueblos *"...the Revolt was a holy war..."*

Robert W. Preucel writes in Chapter 1 that Governor Otermín was forced *"to retreat in ignominy to El Paso..."* He mentions a number of writers who have produced works on the Revolt. How should this event be understood? Was it *"...a single anomalous event...or a broader strategy of indigenous resistance..."*? And what does all this imply in the contemporary world?

Causes for the Revolt would be *"...religious persecution and economic oppression."* Preucel quotes R.E. Twitchell as writing that *"...(e)verywhere the Spaniard was regarded as a tyrant."* The encomienda was little more than a *"system of tyranny."* Other writers, including Andrew Knaut, are quoted.

Dr. David Weber is quoted that *"Pueblo oral traditions have not provided significant insights into the Pueblo Revolt...we must listen to Pueblo voices through Spanish interlocutors."* But Preucel mentions the existence of four Hopi oral history accounts referring to the Revolt. He concludes that *"...one of the reasons for the Revolt was the sexual abuse of Pueblo women by Franciscan priests..."* which is never acknowledged in Spanish documentation. Then he goes on to describe how archaeology has shed light on the Revolt. He concludes that by resisting the Spaniards the Pueblos *"...remade themselves."*

The rest of the chapters are written by the following people:

T.J. Ferguson explores *"the architecture of resistance"* around Zuni when six villages were consolidated into one.

Michael Elliott endeavors to identify missions established after the Vargas colonists returned.

Mark Lycett investigates how Spanish missionary activities *"...created, legitimized, and perpetuated novel social relationships..."* in the Galisteo Basin.

Jeannette Mobley-Tanaka writes that Pueblo people resisted Spanish domination through *"feigned acceptance..."* and the use of *"...rumor and innuendo in order to exert control."* She suggests the cross was also used to represent a bird, a dragonfly, or a star, which represented native rituals.

Barbara Mills writes that Pueblo females used ceramics to express resistance. For example, shifting from *"...glaze-paint to matte-paint...is a deliberate act of breaking with the Spanish association of the earlier tradition."*

Patricia Capone and Robert Preucel observe that ceramics with a motif like *"...the double headed key..."* signifies *"...a commitment to living in accordance with the laws of the ancestors."* New designs could be considered as the *"iconography of resistance."*

Kurt and Cindy Dongoske make a comparison of Spanish documentation and Hopi oral history and rock art.

Mathew Liebmann writes that after the Revolt, Christian symbols took on new Pueblo meanings in what he calls a *"Pueblofication"* process.

Peter Whiteley suggests that people finding refuge in Hopi was in fact an act of resisting Spanish authority. These new immigrants greatly influenced Hopi society to the present day.

Michael Wilcox is concerned with post colonialism pressures that affect Pueblo people to the present day.

Rick Hendricks writes that Vargas victories, in which few warriors died and most escaped, had to do mostly with the *"...use of advanced weaponry, military tactics, and Pueblo auxiliaries by the Spanish."*

Curtis Schaafsma challenges the idea that Apaches and Navajos were enemies of the Pueblo people.

Joseph Henry Suina writes that Pueblo secrecy regarding traditional rituals stems from the Spanish colonial period. He states that pueblos are so much bigger in the western areas than along the Rio Grande River because of *"...demands for land by missionary and civil institutions, encroachment by colonist and settlers, disease, and emigration."*

Preucel concludes that contemporary Pueblo people are *"...heirs to the actions and beliefs of their ancestors and the Revolt remains an important part of their identity."* It must also be kept in mind that each village still has a Christian feast day during which traditional dances are performed, perhaps indicating a blend of cultures.

2005

Sando, Joe S. and Agoyo, Herman (eds.) *PO'PAY: Leader of the First American Revolution.* Santa Fe: Clear Light Publishing, 2005.

The book is comprised of chapters contributed by various writers.

82

Governor Bill Richardson writes in the Foreword that the Pueblo Revolt enabled Amerindians to *"preserve their traditions and way of life... and to reconcile the Spanish and Indian communities... This book will help people understand how this centuries-old culture has been able to continue to exist."*

In the Preface, Herman Agoyo says there is *"...no physical description of Po'pay... his face is as familiar as is the face of any recognizable hero... it has lived in remarkable continuity throughout the history of my Pueblo people."*

Agoyo writes that the first Hispanic settlement... *San Juan de los Caballeros (caballeros is Spanish for "gentlemen")* was so named *"...to symbolize the generosity and hospitality provided by our tribal members."*

When studying history in school and college, Pueblo history was never mentioned. The idea to put Po'pay in Statuary Hall came from Herman's wife, Rachele.

While much history has been written on the Revolt, Po'pay is still an enigma. But he was probably a religious leader. *"The Spanish historical records clearly connect him with the Revolt... His role after the Revolt is unclear."*

In the Introduction the venerable Joe Sando states Po'pay *"...was most likely a war captain, which is a religious office."*

Sando states the Pueblo people aren't one group but rather separate nations. They have three distinct language families: Keresan, Tanoan, and Zunian. Po'pay's genius was to unite these separate nations. Today this is represented by the fact that the Pueblos have *"been able to live on their same land, keep their same languages and traditions, and follow their same religion as they had for centuries...in basically peaceful and harmonious coexistence with the Spanish, Mexican and later American settlers and newcomers..."*

Dr. Alfonso Ortiz writes that the *"Revolution of 1680...was a great act of restoration...of respect for life, peace and freedom by the Pueblo people that was routinely violated by the Spaniards..."*

Ortiz writes that *"...Spaniards had nothing but contempt..."* for the Pueblo gods of peace, brotherhood, mutual respect, and cooperation. The Franciscans burned some 1600 masks. There was disease, drought, and famine, perhaps a sign that the Pueblo gods were displeased with the new ways. The Pueblo people didn't know what caused this new imbalance in the *"harmony of life."* The Spaniards did their utmost to stamp out *"...ancient religious beliefs and practices."*

The second chapter by Dr. Ortiz is titled *"Po'pay's Leadership: A Pueblo Perspective."* He states that *"Spaniards had treated the Pueblo people with consummate arrogance and complete intolerance...no ordinary Pueblo Indian in 17th century New Mexico could own a horse or a gun."*

Who was Po'pay? There are a few clues. Of all the Revolt leaders, he was the only one to be known exclusively by his native name. He was probably a member of the *"...summer moiety and of the summer priesthood, perhaps even the chief priest."* It is likely he was a religious leader. As such, he could not have ordered the murder of Nicolas Bua, his son-in-law, because *"...he could not have taken life of any kind..."*

The three spirits who guided Po'pay were not demons but rather culture heroes named *"Tilini, Tleume, and Caudi."*

Next to nothing is known about Po'pay after 1680 *"...and he was dead before the Spanish resettlement in 1693."*

Spaniards who came to resettle could no longer be so arrogant. They learned to overcome their *"...fear and contempt toward indigenous institutions and beliefs."* In time, *"increasingly native Hispanics and the undeniably Hispanicized Pueblo peoples learned to live and let live."*

Joe S. Sando contributed the chapter titled *"The Pueblo Revolt."* He states that little is known about Po'pay (*"Ripe Cultigens"*). Born in Ohkay Owingeh Pueblo, he might have been about fifty years old, and he was a man of the people, though *"Nothing is known of him before he reached his mature years."*

Sando then goes back to the stories of Alvar Nuñez Cabeza de Vaca, Fray Marcos de Niza, Coronado, and Oñate.

Oñate's settlers began to graze cattle and overgrazing caused *"...soil erosion and the destruction of Pueblo farmland."* This and the drought caused great harm.

The Acoma War "...*created an indelible impression of Spanish cruelty.*" This was reinforced when plains Apaches were slaughtered during the administration of Luis de Rosas (1637-1653).

A constant was the "...*cruel exploitation of Indian labor.*" Indians had to support "...*the Spanish missions, the military forces, and the civil institutions.*"

In the 17th century "...*many Indians died from diseases introduced by the Spanish.*"

Worst of all was religious persecution. Religious customs permeated Pueblo life so Indians finally had to practice their ancient rituals in secret in order to survive.

Bitter feuds between Church and State officials proved "...*the intruders could not even govern themselves.*"

Po'pay and other leaders secretly gathered to discuss a strategy for Pueblo emancipation. "*The Spaniards must be told to leave... or suffer the consequences.*"

Sando then provides what he describes as "...*an imaginative recreation...*" of events leading up to the Revolt. Finally the participants declare, "*We will ask them to leave and if they will leave, let them go peacefully. We will use force only if they refuse.*"

The most hated of the "*blue eyes*" were Francisco Xavier, Luis de Quintana, and Diego Lopez Sombrano. But when the killing started there was no holding back. Twenty-one Franciscans were killed, along with "...*some 400 of the resistant Spaniards.*"

By August 13, some 500 warriors were invading Santa Fe itself. Parleys didn't accomplish anything. Finally the Spaniards charge out of Santa Fe and fight all day, killing some 300 and almost routing the Indians. But more Indians kept arriving so the Christians decided to abandon Santa Fe. The Pueblos didn't attack because "...*there was no need for unnecessary bloodshed.*"

The Pueblo people were now free to live and enjoy their ancient ways. But it appears there were serious problems in Puebloland because in 1683 the leader Luis Tupatú sent a messenger to Governor Otermín saying Hispanics could return to northern New Mexico so long as they were not bent on revenge.

Sando discusses the futile attempts to reconquer New Mexico until the successful entry of Diego de Vargas, which was prepared by certain Pueblo leaders going to El Paso in 1692 to confer with the new governor.

There were other revolts in 1694 and 1696 but now some villages were aligned against others. The Pueblo people were never again united as under Po'pay.

In 1820 the Pueblo people were granted citizenship equal to that of Hispanics. When Mexico took over in 1821, the Mexican government recognized Pueblo citizenship. When the USA took over things changed: in

1855 the Territorial Legislature passed a law that denied Pueblo people the right to vote. In 1948 Miguel Trujillo of Isleta Pueblo went to court and won the right for Pueblo people to vote in American elections.

Sando ends the chapter by saying *"…the Pueblos were most fortunate that it was Spaniards who colonized this area…"* because Pueblo land rights were respected and they were granted full citizenship. Later the Treaty of Guadalupe Hidalgo continued to protect their land holdings but some Pueblo lands were lost because of the American Homestead Act and the Taylor Grazing Act.

The next chapter is written by Theodore S. Jojola and titled *"The Legacy of the Pueblo Revolt & the Tiquex Province."*

The Pueblo Revolt influenced *"…social, economic and political relations…"* for the Pueblo people. The Tiquex Province west of the Sandía and Manzano mountains still remembered the wrath of Coronado. By the time of Oñate the Indians didn't trust Spaniards. Despite previous missionaries being martyred, Franciscans set themselves to saving souls. One of their most impressive achievements was building the Isleta church.

Jojola discusses the nun Maria de Jesus de Agreda and her visitation to the Jumano Indians.

Church and State officials then started fighting with each other. Smallpox took *"…an estimated 3000 natives."* Drought plagued the region. Spaniards were now associated with nothing but trouble. The last straw was Gov. Treviño arresting 47 *sorcerers*. The wheels were now set in motion for the Revolt.

Spanish population was now about 2800 people of which 170 were professional soldiers. Pueblos numbered in the thousands and when the war began even some mestizos joined the attackers. Santa Fe was completely surrounded by warriors and when the water supply was cut off it was just a matter of time before the Hispanic survivors made their way south, where they later linked up with the Hispanos of the Rio Abajo.

Otermín attempted a Reconquest late in 1681. At Isleta Pueblo the governor and his troops were given supplies. Despite the drought, the Isletans had enough food. Other pueblo groups had been threatening to rob them of their foodstuffs. Otermín didn't accomplish a Reconquest.

In 1692 *"…a Pueblo delegation…"* showed up in El Paso and stated the Pueblo people were now fighting each other, hostile nomads were attacking everybody, and the drought was worse than ever. Governor Vargas was invited to return his people to northern New Mexico. Vargas began what is known as the Reconquest.

"…The Pueblo Revolt proved to be a Pyrrhic victory." While Isleta and Sandía

still exist, *"The Piros and Tompiros...no longer exist as distinct cultures."*

The Tiwa communities of Sandía and Isleta are thriving, in part due to Indian gaming operations.

"The Pueblo Revolt was one of the most memorable events in the course of human affairs for the region."

Joseph H. Suina contributed the chapter titled "Underestimation of Pueblo Power." Suina asserts that Pueblo people have been able to keep more of their native culture than any of the tribes in the present USA. This is astounding because they had to survive *"...some of the worst colonial policies and practices directed against any indigenous group on the face of the earth."*

Catholicism was forced on the Pueblos by *"...brute intimidation when necessary..."* Taxation and other types of servitude weighed heavily on the *"...peaceful Pueblo people."* Spaniards became *"...confident, arrogant and despotic..."* but the Pueblos managed to maintain their traditions and religious sites. While uniting against the oppressors was no simple feat, the Pueblos were able to do it because in essence they believed *"Together we live, alone we die."* The group always came before the individual in Pueblo culture. Secrecy was basic for combating the *"hand of tyranny."* This was used in the modern age to thwart the *"Religious Crimes Code and the removal of children to distant boarding schools to uproot their native language and traditions..."* by American authorities.

Today you find Christian feast days in the pueblos, right along with ancient native dances. This gives everyone a sense of worth.

The next chapter, written by Herman Agoyo, is titled "The Tricentennial Commemoration." Agoyo writes that to celebrate the Tricentennial *"...was the fulfillment of a dream."* Once more it united all 19 pueblos. Without the genius of Po'pay there would be no celebration.

The celebration would be one of heritage and Pueblo values. It would promote an understanding of Pueblo culture and traditions.

The celebration started in July of 1980 at San Juan Pueblo, the ancient Ohkay Owingeh. Colorful and sacred dances were performed. There were all kinds of music, traditional and modern. There were footraces for everyone. During the three-day festival people acquired *"...an education on the Pueblo Revolt and its significance."*

On August 9, 1980, an important gathering took place at Santo Domingo, attended by Spanish, Mexican, and State dignitaries, in order to exchange *"...gifts, renew historical ties, and reinforce Pueblo sovereignty recognized by the Spaniards in the 17th century."*

Delfin Lovato of the all Indian Pueblo Council reminded everyone of the *"...atrocities endured by our forefathers under Spanish rule."* De Vargas used *"...extreme and violent measures to again subjugate the Pueblo Indians."* But the Pueblo people knew how *"...to forgive and forget these abuses..."*

Governor Bruce King hosted a gala at the Governor's Mansion, which included Indian dances in honor of the Pueblo people.

Runners recreated *"...the carrying of the knotted cords."* When the runners entered a village there was a *"...feeling of brotherhood and oneness..."*

Part II of the book is titled "The Story of the Statue of Po'pay." It relates facts like how Cliff Fragua was chosen to create the statue, how Senator Manny Aragon and Representative Nick Salazar sponsored Senate Bill 404 to formally nominate Po'pay to be placed in Statuary Hall in Washington D.C., etc.

A Statuary Hall Commission and Foundation was formed for the purpose of appearance of the statue and for fund-raising.

The next section of the book is titled "Controversy Over the Selection of Po'pay." Few people took notice of what was happening in 1997. Controversy reared up in 1998 when Indians protested against a statue of the *brutal* Oñate. Hispanic activists charged, *"Po'pay was equally brutal..."*

Heroes are described as *"...far less than perfect...Their importance lies in the impact of their lives and deeds...In the case of Po'pay we have Pueblo oral history only...which does not discuss Po'pay...but focuses instead on actions and results."* Po'pay enabled the Pueblos *"...to maintain their own lands, languages, customs and religion. Even his detractors can't deny this."*

The Rio Grande Sun newspaper of Española led the movement against Po'pay. Editor/publisher Robert Trapp charged the selection committee might as well have chosen Billy the Kid.

Trapp based his anti-Po'pay comments on Spanish documents, *"...obviously impossible to treat these Spanish sources as unbiased records."* It was pointed out *"...Pueblos have a tradition of maintaining their history orally."*

In 1999 Senator Rod Adair officially proposed replacing Po'pay with someone else. In 2001 Representative Patsy Trujillo Knauer filed another bill to replace Po'pay.

What detractors might not have understood is that *"...Po'pay was being honored less for his personal characteristics than for the achievements of the Pueblo Revolt."*

The concluding chapters relate how Cliff Fragua of Jemez Pueblo was selected to create the sculpture, followed by the "Dedication of the Stone," the "Po'pay Sculpture Takes Shape," "The Unveiling of Po'pay: *Ohkay Owingeh*."

The completed statue is that of a Pueblo man who has been lashed in punishment. His hairstyle is in the Pueblo tradition, bound in a *chongo*. He

87

wears a symbolic necklace around his neck. He holds a knotted cord in his left hand, a bear fetish in the right. A pot behind him symbolizes Pueblo culture. The deerskin he wears signifies his status as provider.

At the May 21, 2005, unveiling at Ohkay Owingeh, *"The statue stood proud."*

2007

Archuleta, Elizabeth. *History Carved in Stone: Memorializing Po'pay and Oñate, or Recasting Racialized Regimes of Representation?* New Mexico Historical Review, Vol. 82, Number 3, Summer 2007, pp. 317-342.

Dr. Archuleta asserts that history has to do with what is remembered and what is forgotten. The majority of statues in Statuary hall *"...celebrates elite white males...ignores non-whites..."* Oñate and Po'pay can be utilized to make the following debate on long-term race relations.

Oñate is lauded as the founder of New Mexico but also condemned by some for his brutal violence. Further, *"...Spanish settlers appropriated Native land and labor..."*

After 1848, Hispanic New Mexicans were *"...racially categorized as white based on a Spanish American identity fabricated in the early twentieth century."* But Anglo Americans considered them racially inferior anyway. There was a controversy over whiteness during which *"Mexican American elites"* tried to distance themselves from people they considered to be inferior: Pueblos, Africans, and nomadic Indians. Claims of whiteness can be said to represent racial superiority or inferiority.

Po'pay represents *"...indigenous struggle, resilience, injustice, and cultural contributions..."* in the Land of Enchantment but also combats white male elitism in Statuary Hall, which in reality connects visitors to *"...the glory rather than the gory in U.S. history."*

The Pueblo Revolt has been written about from Spanish language documentation *"...that ignores other voices and different perspectives."* Pueblo historians like Alfonso Ortiz and Joe Sando have published oral history on the matter.

The Oñate colony had dire consequences for the Pueblos because Spanish cattle *"led to soil erosion, destruction of Pueblo farmland, and crop failures, conditions that did not exist prior to Spanish settlement."*

Elinore M. Barrett is quoted as saying that Pueblo population declined and there was a loss of some fifty (50) pueblos, *"...a loss of 62% of their total number prior to Spanish colonization..."* Also very injurious were the Spanish system of forced tribute, the Pueblo land base was diminished, and trade with other Indian groups was disrupted.

The Pueblos fought back, starting with Acoma in 1598. Acoma was conquered and Oñate *"...decreed that all males over 25 years of age lose their right foot and sentenced them to 20 years of servitude."* This planted *"...seeds of resentment and rage..."* among the Pueblo people.

In 1675 a number of medicine men were arrested and this began the planning for a province wide revolt. When it broke out in August of 1680 over 400 Spanish were killed and some 2000 were sent fleeing to El Paso. They returned twelve years later with Diego de Vargas but the settlers realized *"...they could no longer remain arrogant and intolerant..."*

Archuleta relates how Herman and Rachele Agoyo started a movement to commemorate the Pueblo Revolt and put Po'pay in Statuary Hall. A *"...minor segment..."* of Hispanics protested, which was little more than an effort *"...to replicate inequality and oppression to maintain a New Mexican Spanish/Hispanic identity predicated on whiteness..."*

Opposing Po'pay *"...is tied to contemporary struggles for power and status in New Mexico."* Indians are doing well and this gives them more political power, which enables them to compete with Hispanics. Now Hispanics find themselves having to compete with Indians for social status.

Hispanics started to become *Spanish* when *Anglo Americans* started to settle. Anglos were vastly outnumbered so they worked with elite *Mexican Americans* to achieve the goal of *"whitening up the territory."* Through the use of language and imagination, Mexicans became Spanish Americans, thus being allowed to *"...claim whiteness within the American context of white supremacy."* This also excluded Pueblo Indians, thus destroying the Hispano-Pueblo alliance forged earlier in New Mexican history.

Claims of whiteness are at the base of Oñate supporters who oppose Po'pay. Spanish colonists are portrayed as benevolent people who brought civilization and a rich Spanish heritage to the Indians.

Oñate statues in El Paso and Alcalde are intended *"...to celebrate exclusively the Southwest's Spanish heritage."* Opposition to the El Paso statue, the largest bronze in the USA, resulted in a name change. In Alcalde the director of the Oñate Monument and Visitors Center, Estevan Arellano, said that the foot cutting happened 400 years ago and people are still holding a grudge?! At the same time Arellano said he opposed Po'pay because he murdered priests as well as women and children.

Archuleta states Hispanics still remember the Pueblo Revolt, *"...which also took place four centuries ago..."* Further, Oñate enslaved the indigenous people of Zacatecas, which is how he got to be one of the richest mine owners in the Americas.

Oñate proponents, many of whom are Po'pay opponents *"...rely on the rhetorical strategies of erasure and minimization..."* to portray the effects of

Spanish colonization. Negatives affecting native people are ignored.

"Evidence of erasure surfaced in 1991..." when Millie Santillanes, *"...who traces her ancestry to the original Spanish colonists,"* lobbied to declare 1998 as the Oñate Cuartocentenario to commemorate the 400th anniversary of the founding of Hispanic New Mexico. Santillanes had supporters like the Hispano Chamber of Commerce, the New Mexico Genealogical Association, and the New Mexican Hispanic Culture Preservation League. There was much opposition from various quarters because of *"...the devastating experiences of American Indians...[and] the Acoma experience..."* Santillanes declared it was time to honor the good and forgive the bad. Opposition continued and in the end the Albuquerque Arts Board voted to emphasize all the settlers instead of just Oñate.

New Mexican descendants of Spanish colonists are in reality trying to achieve a racial advantage in contemporary society. This requires that *"...obvious Spanish cruelty against and exploitation of Pueblo Indians..."* be minimized or erased.

The New Mexican Hispanic Culture Preservation League (NMHCPL) is working for minimization by promoting certain programs *"...which exclusively present a Spanish perspective..."* in the schools. Whether or not Spanish settlers did good things for the Indians *"...is beside the point."* Spanish policy was built around the belief in the inferiority of American Indians and mixed bloods. This was and is ludicrous because Oñate himself was married to a woman who had Aztec blood, thus making her a mestiza. So much for *"...the Spanish blood Hispanics claim as pure..."*

Some Anglo and Hispanic politicians, like Rod Adair and Patsy Trujillo-Knauer, tried to suggest other historical figures to honor instead of Po'pay, to no avail.

"...Descendants of the Hispanic elite..." have tried to honor their ancestors while they *"...expunge or diminish the Pueblos' experiences..."* Samuel Delgado *"...orchestrated a strategy to dehumanize Po'pay..."* whereby Hispanics are the victims of Pueblo aggression. Max de Aragon brings up that what is happening is merely evidence that the Black Legend is still present. Conchita Lucero points out there were many instances of Indian cruelty to other Indians. Rubén Sálaz Márquez *"...refers to the revolt as the St. Lawrence Day Massacre, a name with sinister undertones"* and portrays Hispanics as victims of genocide while Spanish violence and killing is masked.

All these efforts are trying to silence Pueblo voices describing the Revolt and its causes. New Mexico's Spanish heritage is promoted as *"...romantic, noble, and honorable..."* which clouds the record of violence against Indians. Further, the *"...story centers on Spanish males and the Spanish upper class..."* which works to *"...preserve white, male-dominated racial identities."*

A *"vocal minority"* considers Oñate to be a great man but under scrutiny one recognizes *"...the brutality and hardships of Spanish colonization..."* Pueblo *"...unity, spirituality, and dignity made them resilient...and resistant to efforts at Hispanicization."*

In November of 2005 the University of New Mexico held a Po'pay Commemoration Symposium to celebrate Cliff Fragua's sculpture being installed in Washington D.C. Pueblo scholars spoke. Elena Ortiz-Junes compared the Revolt to other important events in American history. She states that Po'pay was fighting for many of the ideas expressed in the Declaration of Independence and the Emancipation Proclamation.

State Historian Dr. Estevan Rael-Galvez said that history should be more than mere dates. It should include *"...everyday acts of courage like the Pueblos' bravery in engaging the Spanish enemy..."*

Sculptures of Oñate and Po'pay might force viewers to equate the importance of these historical personalities. Pueblo survival is proof to the contrary. Po'pay and Pueblo history will not be erased. Po'pay worked for the people much like *"...George Washington, Thomas Jefferson, and Abraham Lincoln..."* because he *"...fought to free Pueblo communities from Spanish tyranny and to keep Indian nations united."* The Revolt *"...ended the persecutions and secured the future of the Pueblos – their culture, their land rights, and their religious freedom."*

Part IX
Analysis and Conclusions

~

IN 1971 DR. PHILIP WAYNE POWELL PUBLISHED HIS BOOK *Tree of Hate* in which he describes how northern Europeans created the *Black Legend* of anti-Spanish propaganda and prejudice that has become basic in some schools of European and American history. Dr. Powell asserts that *Tree of Hate* propaganda can be found from the American elementary school through the college classroom, *"...from romantic to prosaic and from near sublime to thoroughly ridiculous."* Powell believes the Black Legend is an erroneous view of Spain, its people, and its Church.

92   It will be observed that four of the five works discussed in the Review above are affiliated with universities. Perhaps Powell is correct when he says the Black Legend still *"...echoes in today's university classrooms"*?

The work by Robert Silverberg is clearly in the *Tree of Hate* category. When he says that *the martyrdom of the Indians at the hands of Spain was one of history's darkest episodes* he is implying that all was negative and nothing was positive, which is mere pandering to popular prejudice. Powell refers to this type of historiography as *"...a witches brew of truth, half-truth, propaganda, prejudice, and political expediency."*

Spaniards recorded everything so the conquest and pacification of the Americas is the best-documented period in all of history until the 19th century. Further, Spaniards recorded *both sides* of every issue, which some writers have used to the detriment of truth. For example, the greatest of civil rights workers in the history of the Americas was Bartolomé de las Casas. He labored mightily for justice and wrote against the atrocities that were taking place. He demanded reform and was successful. But his writing has been used to prove how terrible the Spanish were instead of how they struggled to be humane. This Orwellian approach to the history of Spain in the Americas isn't uncommon.

It is historical fact that Spanish atrocities were severely criticized by fearless, articulate, powerful clergymen like Las Casas. And the historical record proves that the Spanish Crown listened. For example, see *The Spanish Struggle for Justice in the Conquest of America* by Lewis Hanke. He states:

> *No other European people, before or since the conquest of America, plunged into such a struggle for justice as developed among Spaniards... Ecclesiastics...influence was felt in all quarters and ensured that every basic decision made during the conquest be scrutinized from the point of view of Christian justice...Religiosity was an integral and vital part of Spanish life...Some conquistadores were at times as missionary minded as the most devoted friars. A few ecclesiastics were as worldly as Pizarro...It is to Spain's everlasting credit that she allowed men to insist that all her actions in America be just, and that at times she listened to those voices.*

Powell is among those writers who reject the idea that Spaniards were uniquely cruel, rapacious, greedy, or depraved. He asserts Spanish achievements rested more on diplomacy than on war. The classic example is Cortés in Mexico. He obtained the allies he needed by relying on astute diplomatic skills. Indeed, it can be stated with complete accuracy that Mexican Aztecs were conquered by Spanish led Mexican Indians who, the truth be told, hated the Aztecs. And there are other examples, like Vargas in New Mexico. 93

So where is Robert Silverberg getting his information that *"All Acoma males had a foot chopped off before twenty years of servitude"* and that there were *"...orchards of fruit unfamiliar to the Pueblos...pears, peaches, figs, dates, pomegranates, olives, cherries, quinces, lemons, oranges, nectarines"* in the Acoma area? Common sense is enough to rebut such assertions but a university press published the work anyway.

The work by Dr. Andrew Knaut appeared in 1995. He states that Spanish language documentation *"reflects all too faithfully the biases of Spanish observers."* But even a quick look at his book shows that he quoted Spanish documents, or at least researchers who translated Spanish language documents, whenever they were negative, when Spaniards were criticizing other Spaniards. These he presented as *valid documentation,* not *"biases of Spanish observers."* Incidentally, it is doubtful that Dr. Knaut translated Spanish language documents himself to use in his work. On page 113 he writes: *"They brought him a mestizo woman..."* Anyone with knowledge of Spanish would say *mestiza,* not *mestizo woman,* which is like saying a *male female* in English.

Dr Knaut writes that Spanish policy was based on *intimidation.* As proof he cites the Acoma foot cutting for all men over twenty-five years of age. Historian Marc Simmons writes in his *The Last Conquistador,* based on the extensive work on Oñate by Hammond and Rey, that the sentence was directed at *twenty-four* (24) warriors. So whom do you believe, Knaut or Simmons? Was Dr. Knaut not aware of the monumental Hammond and Rey work? Did Dr. Knaut not realize that no one ever recorded seeing a footless Indian in New Mexico?

Knaut blames the Spanish for injecting turmoil into Pueblo society. Does he understand that the Pueblos were not one society? Neither was there constant peace between these different people who were perpetually involved in alliance and counter-alliance. Self-defense was always a necessity, which is why the people moved into villages in the first place.

Knaut and other writers make much of feuds between New Mexican Church and State officials. Were these officials any worse in scope than the contemporary fights between Republicans and Democrats? Didn't President Richard Nixon resign from the presidency before he was impeached? Weren't impeachment charges brought against President Bill Clinton? How many congressmen have resigned in disgrace? Should we judge what is happening to the USA by what transpires in the presidency or Congress?

It appears to be popular to write that Hispanics mixed with Pueblos, though Knaut says, *"No quantitative data exists."* If no data exists then how can Dr. Knaut project (what he refers to as) miscegenation? Further, does Dr. Knaut understand that only government officials could live in an Indian village? So what would have been the frequency for racial mixing? And do a few Amerindians out of a hundred Hispanic ancestors prove racial mixing? Yes, if you are a *"one drop makes you an Indian"* racist, which is more a product of American racism than Spanish colonial society in New Mexico. For example, in some parts of the later USA, miscegenation was against written laws. There were no such laws in New Mexico.

It is a popular misconception that Spanish women didn't come to the new world. Dr. Powell has written:

After 1500, ships and fleets...regularly carried Spanish women, children, servants [to the New World]...On the farthest frontiers, even when Spaniards first arrived, Spanish women and families commonly accompanied their men, facing all the dangers and hardships...we usually underrate the fortitude and adventurous spirit of Spanish women and their loyalty to their men..."

He calls for studies to be made and books to be written about women in the conquest and colonization of the Americas. As far as I know, the work hasn't been done in the English language.

A constant theme by Knaut and other writers is how the Spanish made the Pueblo people *suffer*. One might well ask if Spaniards did anything other than persecute the Pueblos, or how the Pueblos *survived*, such was the *oppression*. But no comparison is made to the Indians on the east coast, who didn't survive under the English. And it would be treasonous to bring up policies like the deportation of all Indians from east of the Mississippi by the *heroic* Andrew Jackson, President of the United States. Is that why *patriotic* writers are targeting Spain? Is it possible that writers are trying to cover up American treatment of Indians by projecting American atrocities on Spaniards? If we were to write a comparative history, what would be the result?

Dr. Knaut writes that Governor Treviño constantly persecuted Po'pay. How would this be possible when Po'pay wasn't even identified until after the Revolt broke out? How could he have been persecuted when Spanish authorities or missionaries didn't even know of his existence? So is Dr. Knaut promoting propaganda under the guise of History?

Upon reading *Archaeologies of the Pueblo Revolt: Identity, Meaning, and Renewal in the Pueblo World,* one might easily deduce that just about everything the Pueblo people did was related to the Revolt. (It has often been said that academics write to impress each other. The scholarship in the various articles is certainly impressive so long as you have a penchant for interpretation.) Editor Robert Preucel does bring up an issue, perhaps unintentionally, that must be addressed: cultural forces from outside New Mexico are influencing Pueblo people. Herman Agoyo freely admits he was unaware that 1980 would be the 300th anniversary of the Pueblo Revolt until someone from the Smithsonian Institution told him about it. So it can be said that the *Po'pay movement* is in reality inspired by outsiders, not Pueblo New Mexicans.

It has also been observed that some individuals come to towns like Santa Fe from American areas where the Indians were brutally exterminated or later deported to Oklahoma, they find Indians here who have been preserved by Hispanic society, so these individuals now become *champions of the Indians,* very willing to defend them *against New Mexican Hispanics,* who preserved them in the first place. One might well ask if they were champions back where they came from, especially if anti-Indian bias still exists, as in Oklahoma.

Of special interest to writers of History is the lack of Pueblo oral history concerning Po'pay and the twelve years Hispanics were out of northern New Mexico. If the 1540 atrocities of Coronado can be remembered, along with Oñate's 1599 *"hacking off one foot of Acoma males,"* why don't collective memory and oral history tell us about Po'pay and the twelve subsequent years after 1680? Someone will have to answer this question because none of the authors mentioned in the Review above have been able to cite Pueblo

95

oral history regarding Po'pay and the Revolt. Well-known historians like Dr. David Weber have remarked on this matter. It appears everything known is based on written Spanish language documentation.

It would appear that referring to the Revolt as *"the first American Revolution"* is another example of influence from outside New Mexico. The phrase wasn't in book print, as far as I know, before the Clear Light Publishing *PO'PAY* volume edited by Joe Sando and Herman Agoyo. And in this work, once again there is an admission that there is no oral history information on Po'pay and the years after 1680. Spanish documents are the only source of information.

As already mentioned, the translation of Spanish language documents is crucial. Translation errors promote invalid history. For example, *San Juan de los Caballeros* should be translated as *Knights of St. John,* not *St. John of the Gentlemen,* where the people of San Juan received the new settlers "with hospitality," the impression being that the people of Okhay Owingeh were the *gentlemen.*

Religious persecution of the Pueblos is a constant in this and other books in the Review. No author explains Pueblo religious beliefs for an outsider to understand. Was the Eagle Dance a manifestation of Pueblo religion? The *Buffalo Dance?* The *Rain Dance* that utilized snakes? How about dancing with scalps taken from enemies? Or are these the dances outsiders are permitted to observe, reserving true religious dances for private celebration? These questions haven't been answered.

If anything is known about the Revolt it is that it came as a surprise so how can anyone assert *"The Spaniards must be told to leave"* or *"We will ask them to leave"* or *"We will use force only if they refuse"*? The Spanish New Mexicans who were slaughtered were never advised to leave before they were attacked on their farms and ranches.

Historical facts prove that most of the dead were innocent noncombatants like women and children. The *"hated Francisco Xavier, Luis de Quintana, and Diego Lopez Sombrano"* were not casualties, proving once again that it is ordinary people who pay the price for revolution, not the people who cause it. Around three out of every four dead were women and children, yet we are told that *"...some 400 of the resistant Spaniards"* had to be killed. Until now, no one has asked how women and children resisted.

The only real battle of the Revolt took place when warriors were attacking Santa Fe. Hispanos, less than a hundred in number, charged out to do combat. After fierce fighting the Indians scurried to safety in the hills until reinforcements arrived from other Pueblos. Despite overwhelming numbers, the Indians didn't attack again because now they had faced Spanish fighting men instead of unsuspecting farm and ranch people. When the water supply was cut off there was no choice but to abandon Santa Fe. The thousands of Indians still didn't attack and the caravan of refugees made its way south to safety. The fact that there was no attack is often interpreted as due to the *peaceful nature* of Pueblo Indians, not that Spaniards were now ready to fight.

Pueblo *"freedom from Spanish oppression"* evidently wasn't working out because by 1683 the new Pueblo leader Luis Tupatú sent a messenger to Gov. Otermín with the message that Hispanos could return if they didn't exact revenge. Another Pueblo delegation did the same thing in 1692. Historians haven't emphasized these significant realities. If Hispanics were being invited back, perhaps they weren't the oppressors some historians have represented them to be?

The way American historiography is written is a constant in how information is presented to students of New Mexico history. One might well ask why historians have neglected to explore or publicize the fact that Pueblo people were given Spanish citizenship in 1820. When Mexico took over in 1821, Pueblo citizenship was again recognized until the USA came in and took it away, another fact that American historians have not publicized. Indeed, the only one to bring it out is Native American historian Joe Sando.

Franciscan missionaries in New Mexico have been criticized more than lauded for laboring to bring Christianity to Native Americans. American historians have generally emphasized missionaries forcing the Indians to become Catholics and being intolerant of Native religious practice. If we were to do a comparative study we would find that the English on the east coast didn't make significant efforts to bring Indians into the Christian fold. They weren't considered worthy of Christianization. Extermination proved to be English policy. During the Pontiac War of 1763, Lord Jeffrey Amherst gave the Indians smallpox infested blankets in order to kill them off because he believed Indians were *"an execrable race"* whose *extermination would be a service to mankind*. But no such comparative history has been written. And if it was, would it find a publisher?

97

Despite activities that today are considered abuses, the Pueblo people of New Mexico survived basically intact with their religion, cultures, languages, and land holdings. This needs to be emphasized because it didn't happen anywhere else. England and the USA don't begin to compare with Spain and Mexico when it comes to humanitarian Indian policy, but American historians would pay a big price for saying that, if the work got published.

Contemporary Pueblo celebrations are indeed festive affairs in which everyone is welcome. Dancers no longer carry snakes or human scalps but other native dances have continued without interruption. Now there is a Po'pay celebration complete with runners carrying knotted cords. This is ritual perhaps, acceptable so long as people are unaware of the slaughter which they could be said to represent. Are there such celebrations east of the Mississippi? Certainly there are no runners carrying smallpox infected blankets.

In the western USA there are no celebrations commemorating the Amerindian victims of the Council House Massacre in San Antonio, the Washita massacre in Oklahoma, the Sand Creek massacre in Colorado, the Camp Grant massacre in Arizona, or the brutal extermination of California Indians. Realizing this historical fact, why is the Pueblo Revolt so celebrated?

Dr. Elizabeth Archuleta might well ask why the above have been ignored but her attention seems to be riveted on Spanish New Mexico. There is no denying that "white males" comprise the ruling class in American as well as New Mexican society but charges of brutality focus on New Mexico, not the American West. [Would the *New Mexico Historical Review* accept an article for publication if a Sand Creek atrocity had taken place in New Mexico?]

There is no doubt that Americans of the 19th century were products of a racist culture. Dr Archuleta accepts and perpetuates the racist tradition by referring to Americans as *"Anglos,"* as if Americans were all from England (although English people refer to themselves as *Brits*). She brings up people who claim to be *pure Spanish* but she never gets close to mentioning an investigation of those who claim to be *pure Anglo*.

Americans who came into New Mexico were from many different ethnic groups but in order to pretend to be dominant they referred to themselves as *Anglos* as a rallying strategy against overwhelming Hispanic numbers. The practice continues to the present day so we find German Anglos, Yugoslavian Anglos, Italian Anglos, Polish Anglos, etc. Ironically, the strategy has been quite successful because most people use *Anglo* as if it was a single ethnic group. Of course, this is not done in areas outside New Mexico or the Southwest. It is certain that someone in Boston claiming to be superior because he is *Anglo* would be laughed out of town.

People living in frontier New Mexico, a period more or less from 1598 until about 1890, were quite democratic in their views of equality, especially when hostile Indians were attacking. They didn't worry about bloodlines if someone was willing to help them survive. This relatively egalitarian frontier society must be taken into account when discussing race or ethnic relations in New Mexico. Despite typical European notions on race and racial superiority, frontier New Mexico could never compare to the USA for racism. For example, in the American South it was illegal even to teach an African to read or to write. In New Mexico there was a definite effort to teach Spanish to the Indians.

98

There is no doubt that some Hispanos in New Mexico were concerned with being considered Caucasian. For better or for worse, this is part of the European heritage. (Europeans have always considered themselves superior and it is no rarity to meet Europeans today who consider themselves superior to Americans.) But Dr. Archuleta is wrong to believe the idea of being Spanish began with the American entry into New Mexico. According Dr. John Kessell and researchers in the Vargas Project, many of the Vargas colonists were *Spanish* in their declarations and acknowledged as such in the community in which they lived.

These Spanish colonists evolved into what came to be called *Spanish-Americans,* possibly to differentiate themselves from newly arrived immigrants from Mexico. Were they *pure* Spanish? Who cares and how would one prove it anyway without serious, expensive DNA testing for all descendants? Such a question only concerns racists who don't accept that all human beings have mixed bloodlines if you go back far enough. Modern genome testing has verified that human beings across the planet Earth have 99.9% the exact same DNA.

Most people agree that New Mexicans have never been frightened by diversity. What must be kept in mind is that these *Spanish people* entered human society through Spanish forms found on the New Mexican frontier. Are New Mexican Hispanos *purebloods?* That is merely a racist fixation in the present day that can be answered in whatever way one wishes, especially since people from all over the globe somehow become *Anglos* in New Mexico. So why is it acceptable to be *Anglo* but not *Spanish?* Has anyone ever bothered to investigate if someone is *pure Anglo?* That is ludicrous but often demanded of people describing themselves as *Spanish.*

It is ludicrous to believe that opposing Po'pay being placed in Statuary Hall *"...is a struggle for power and status...and whiteness."* If someone like Pablo Abeita from Isleta had been selected there would never have been controversy, I would wager. Hispano New Mexicans don't have a history of resenting Indians, historically or presently. If there had existed significant animosity the Indians would have been exterminated after the atrocities of the Revolt. Historic alliances with the Pueblos and the Comanches will attest to that fact. What people who know New Mexican history resent is the slaughter of some 300 women and children that Po'pay represents.

Were the Franciscans vile because they wanted to Christianize Indians and impart European civilization? (Are Americans vile for wanting to spread *democracy?*) While they sometimes failed they were very successful most of the time. Was this good or bad? The reader can decide but this should be done with sufficient study as a background. Lewis Hanke quotes Fernando de los Ríos on this matter:

99

Let us judge the Spanish colonial activities, not as Catholics or Protestants, but as observers with the objectivity necessary to one who proposes to study a problem of great significance in history.

Pueblo people and their achievements are a big factor in the contemporary New Mexico tourist industry. This is good for everyone concerned and there is no one who would change it. By the same token, few would assert that the New Mexican Spanish heritage has been promoted as it should be to attract more tourism. Indeed, Hispanics have been more ignored or denigrated than lauded. This could be dismissed as a case of self-pity so let's elucidate: why has no recreation ever been made of the Knights of St. John (*San Juan de los Caballeros*) settlement? Or of San Gabriel? It has been done for visitors to the later Williamsburg, Virginia, and Plymouth Plantation, but not for tourists in New Mexico.

The charge of Spanish cruelty against the Indians is common but when is it ever said that the Pueblo people were preserved *because of the Spanish?* The Pueblos did it on their own because of their native traditions? Their traditions wouldn't have deflected bullets or cannon balls if they had been aimed their way.

Extermination or deportations were not Spanish policy but how often is that articulated? How many people, including Ph.D.s, can talk intelligently about the Hispano alliance with Pueblos and Comanches?

Hispanic people created what later would be copied and become known as the ranching and mining *American West* but when do we hear that?

Robert Denhardt has written that the greatest horsemen *in the history of the world* have been the Arabs, the Comanches, and the Hispanos of New Mexico. Is that being taught in the schools? You can certainly believe the *foot cutting* is being taught, without applying the common sense observation that what good would a footless Indian do on a farm or ranch.

Squash blossom jewelry and the outdoor "Indian oven" are considered Indian in the popular mind but they are in fact Spanish contributions to New Mexican culture. The missionaries taught natives how to create the squash blossom and the *horno* oven is a product of wheat culture, which didn't exist in New Mexico before Hispanics arrived. Incidentally, the Pueblos didn't have chile either. This was brought in by Hispanos, a gift from the Indians of Mexico the Pueblos didn't have before Hispanos arrived.

To bring us into the American period, the New Mexican civil rights record is better than anywhere else in the USA. For example it can be said with historical accuracy that there has never been a race riot in New Mexico begun by Amerindians or Hispanics.

Why is it that statues of Oñate are so denigrated? Why is it that a statue of Elfego Baca stands in out-of-the-way Reserve, New Mexico, instead of tourist centers like Taos, Santa Fe, Albuquerque, or Las Cruces? Baca was involved in the greatest gunfight in the West when he single-handedly fought off some 84 Texas cowboys who were trying to kill him for arresting one of their own. Why isn't Baca lauded? Perhaps because Hispanics are promoted as the *villains of New Mexico?* Is that good for tourism? Is it good for young people growing up in New Mexico?

Dr. Archuleta writes that the 1680 Revolt *"...took place four centuries ago..."* And this statement got by the editors of the *New Mexico Historical Review,* a scholarly publication. Incidentally, to my knowledge the Historical Review has never published an item on the Hispanic victims of the Pueblo Revolt. An article submitted by Luis Brandtner on this matter was rejected by the NMHR.

Dr. Archuleta focuses her invective on the New Mexican Hispanic Culture Preservation League and some of its members. The charge is that wanting to commemorate the 400th anniversary of the founding of Hispanic New Mexico *"...is a strategy of erasure..."* against Indians. As a founding member of the League I can say that nothing could be further from the truth. At the behest of Millie Santillanes, people got together to combat the defamation of Hispanics who made history and the effects such denigration has in the present day. "Minimization" of Indians had nothing to do with creating the League. The organization's Mission Statement reads as follows: 101

The Mission of the New Mexican Hispanic Culture Preservation League is to preserve the heritage, Spanish language and history of Hispanic New Mexico; to promote the education and understanding of the contri-butions of Hispanics to the development of New Mexico and the nation; and to protect the history of the New Mexican Hispanic heritage and culture. To achieve this mission, we will seek the truth of our heritage and history and restore the pride and honor of our New Mexican Hispanic culture.

As can be seen, the organization is anti-ignorance, not anti-Indian or anti-American or anti-anything else. Even casual research would uncover that fact.

Incidentally, all that was asked for to celebrate 1998 was a bust of Oñate. Despite the controversy or perhaps because of it, Albuquerque's Old Town got *La Jornada* (The Journey) *Memorial,* one of the largest bronze sculptures in the country.

CONCLUSIONS

Let us point out the reality that *The Pueblo Revolt Massacre* is the only item of its kind in that no other book has been written from the point of view of the victims who died in the so-called Pueblo Revolt. While Hackett's monumental work is generally available in Special Collections sections of large libraries, until now there has been no popular read to compete with the items discussed in the above Review of the Literature section. One might well ask why this is so because so much has been written about New Mexico up to this point in time. Why not the victims of the Pueblo Revolt?

Have publishers not found the *massacre* perspective worthy of interest? Is it that they don't want further to antagonize Indian communities that generally were dealt with so criminally by England and the USA? Worse still, would it be tantamount to cultural treason to publish a book like *The Pueblo Revolt Massacre?*

Perhaps it is a simple matter of dollars and cents. Is it a better business investment to promote *persecuted Indians* fighting *Spanish tyranny?* Now that there is no more frontier populated by hostile Indians, it is a New Mexican reality that Pueblo Indians *sell* so this would dictate an emphasis on the Pueblos. The only villains left...are Hispanics? So is it a de facto policy to laud Pueblo Indians and vilify *the Spanish* in New Mexico?

102

HISPANOS in SANTA FE

Santa Fe has been described by some as very pro-Pueblo Indian and a hot-bed of anti-Hispanic racism. Has Santa Fe developed into an anti-Hispanic, anti-Catholic town, despite its native Hispano population? Is it true that Hispanic history and culture is virtually ignored? For example, there is much more to the culture than Santero Art, which is certainly a popular item in town museums but which is only part of the many contributions of Hispanic New Mexico.

There can be no denying that culture is big in *"the City Different."* Culture is part of the Santa Fe allure and mystique, which includes a dominating Indian presence year round and especially during the yearly Indian Market. For example, the *Indian Market* publication (published by the *Santa Fe New Mexican* newspaper) of some 185 pages (in 2007) contains some articles but mostly advertisements from Santa Fe art galleries and various businesses catering especially to visitors. The *Santa Fean* magazine (some 224 pages in August of 2007) has an issue devoted strictly to the Indian Market event. This issue has articles but also much advertising. Pueblo Indians are promoted everywhere, perhaps because they can't be found in most tourist centers outside New Mexico.

Indian vendors under the porch of the Palace of the Governors are an ever-popular attraction. Museums are replete with Indian items and most tourists find them fascinating, which is all to the good. After all, where most tourists come from east of the Mississippi, Indians were either exterminated or deported to Oklahoma.

It can't be forgotten that Santa Fe was and continues to be an important part of New Mexico's Hispanic heritage as well as the heart of the contemporary tourism industry. Granted there is also a Spanish Market publication, a magazine containing forty-two (42) pages in 2007, also printed by the *Santa Fe New Mexican* newspaper. (This publication has more articles but also some advertising.) Should the *Market* publications be compared?

Is Santa Fe capitalizing on its Hispanic heritage? What is the designated role for New Mexico's Hispano history and culture in the entire New Mexico tourist industry? These questions deserve to be answered then scrutinized by the State Legislature, at least those who don't have an *Above-It-All* attitude. It must be asked if minimizing the Hispanic heritage is a way to neutralize the influence of a large Hispanic population.

Some observations can certainly be made. The year 1998 was the 400th anniversary of settlement of Spanish New Mexico. The Office of Cultural Affairs and *New Mexico Magazine* each put out a calendar every year, as they did in 1998. *Their 1998 calendars didn't even mention the 400th anniversary of the founding of Hispanic New Mexico.* Would this tend to indicate that Hispanos, in or out of Santa Fe, are being ignored, at least by some State government agencies based in Santa Fe?

MUSEUM of NEW MEXICO

There has been no confrontation as occurred in 2001 when the Museum of New Mexico put up a picture of a bikini-clad female with a *Lady of Guadalupe* background. The mockery went up despite a member of the Board of Directors advising the Museum that it would cause a storm of protest because the Virgin of Guadalupe is considered by Catholics to be the Patroness of the Americas. (Some people went to the Governor and demanded the dissenting Board member be removed from his post.)

So the bikini item went up, there were vigorous protests from the Catholic community, a guard had to be stationed by the picture to protect it, and the Museum refused to take it down, *the Catholic community be damned.*

Legislators asked for the removal of the mockery but defenders stated it was a matter of *freedom of speech.* The Museum of New Mexico saw to it that the exhibit ran its scheduled course, though it did discuss the matter with the Archbishop.

When the Bill Richardson administration came in, the new director of the Office of Cultural Affairs, Ruben Smith, fired the Director of the

103

Museum of New Mexico. Various individuals from in and around Santa Fe went to Governor Richardson and demanded that Smith be fired or they would work against all funding for the Museum. Richardson caved in to the pressure and fired Smith.

No one could possibly deny that the Museum of New Mexico has the most excellent of museums for all visitors. With the above in mind, it is also proper to investigate as to the exhibits put up in years past by, for example, the Palace of the Governors, and what emphasis is given to New Mexico's Hispano founding pioneers whose descendants are in Santa Fe and New Mexico to this day.

Has the Museum of New Mexico system created an exhibit on governors like Oñate, Vargas, Vélez Cachupín, and Anza? How about an exhibit on pioneering Spanish women from doña Eufemia to Millie Santillanes? Famous missionaries and priests? Sheep husbandry in New Mexico? Sheep kings? *Ciboleros* (the magnificent buffalo lancers)? *Mesteñeros* (wild horse cowboys)? *Comancheros* (traders who went out on the Great Plains to trade)? *Carreteros* (freighters of the day)? New Mexican horsemen (who have been ranked among the greatest horsemen in the world along with the Arabs and Comanches)? The Hispano/Pueblo alliance (the greatest Euro-Amerindian alliance in the history of what is now the USA)? The Hispano/Comanche alliance (the second greatest Euro-Amerindian alliance in the history of what is now the USA)? The Comanche Peace? New Mexico as a centuries-long frontier society? The supply caravan? New Mexican ranching and mining? *Trovadores* (poets who could create spontaneous rhymed verse)? Spanish language newspapers? Hispanic writers from the missionaries to the present day? Hispanic musicians and their bands? The 200th Coast Artillery and the 515 Coast Artillery? New Mexicans in the Bataan Death March? Medal of Honor recipients from New Mexico? If these exhibits have been created at the Palace of the Governors, they have not been publicized. And what conclusion might be reached if the Palace or the Museum system has had no such focus?

Is the Museum of New Mexico a purveyor of anti Hispanic racism? To my knowledge, no Hispanic has ever been selected to serve as Director. It would be interesting to investigate who holds the high paying positions and who holds the low paying jobs in the Museum system. The New Mexico Legislature might well look into this situation.

In all honesty, it must also be observed that some individuals in the Hispanic groups are as mercurial or anti-Hispanic as anybody else. The only thing Hispanic about them appears to be their Spanish surname. Further, their actions have proved they will combat Hispanic issues just as easily as any skinhead racist.

104

I can speak from personal experience. My book *New Mexico: A Brief Multi-History* was derailed from publication at the National Hispanic Culture Center (NHCC) because of the machinations of a couple of staffers who disinformed the newly hired director Eugene Matta, who then took the disinformation to the Ed Lujan Board of Directors, who cancelled its publication despite already having spent $43,000 on it. (Director Matta didn't mention the situation when he was forced to resign as Director.) Consequently, there were some people in the public at large who came to believe the work was thrown out because it was historically inaccurate, which was the exact opposite of the truth, as events would prove.

The book was printed and well received by the general public. Some legislators sponsored a bill to declare the *Multi-History* the official volume of New Mexico's 400th celebration anniversary. The State Historian, an Hispanic who had been one of the manuscript reviewers at the National Hispanic Culture Center, sent a representative to the hearings to testify against the book's adoption to commemorate the anniversary.

In time the work was submitted for review for use in the public schools. The reviewers, individuals whom I had never met, recommended approval and the *Multi-History* is now being used as a basic text in a number of school districts around the State. In time it was also excerpted into the New Mexico *Blue Book,* New Mexico's official State publication. The work is now in its second printing and available in hardback, all of which started with the Ed Lujan Board of Directors throwing it out of the National Hispanic Culture Center, though not a single Board member read the manuscript, relying totally on the disinformation supplied to them by the two staffers.

When Governor Bill Richardson appointed me to the NHCC Board of Directors a motion was made and passed for me to develop a series of framed historical photographs, which came to be known as the History Gallery. I located donors who paid for the individual framed photographs, twenty-one in number, as it turned out. Despite having been approved by the Board of Directors, the history director refused to put them on display for the public and in time I withdrew them from the NHCC. The History Gallery has since been put on display at the Bataan Military Museum in Santa Fe, the New Mexican Hispanic Culture Preservation League's banquet, the South Broadway Cultural Center in Albuquerque, and the Internet Express-Cyber Café in Albuquerque's South Valley.

When I heard the Center for Regional Studies at the University of New Mexico bought books for libraries around the State, I submitted the *Multi-History* and my new effort, *EPIC of the Greater Southwest,* for their review, since their purported primary mission was to educate people on New Mexico and the Southwest borderlands. Despite the books being written by a native

New Mexican/Southwesterner, with native perspectives not usually found in other such books, the director rejected distributing the books, though he didn't say they were not good for State libraries. Ironically, in August of 2007 the Daughters of the American Revolution bought hundreds of the *Multi-History* books for distribution to school libraries around the State.

CHICANO STUDIES

Dr. Powell has mentioned that university classrooms have spewed out Black Legend propaganda in the past. Since the publication of his *Tree of Hate* in 1971 there has been a tremendous growth in Chicano Studies departments in universities across the country. At the beginning of the movement some "militant" Chicanos promoted the idea of taking the Southwest away from the USA and returning it to Mexico. In these days of terrorists and terrorist threats, Chicanos no longer espouse any such action.

The term *Chicano* is of 20th century coinage and doesn't exist in any historical document that I know of. Denver activist Corky Gonzales created the term *Aztlán* and somehow interpreted it as the Chicano homeland, around 1970, though it doesn't include the concept of emanating from Siberia, which is where Amerindian people migrated from, according to anthropologists. If emphasis is on the *indigenous people,* are Chicano Studies courses anti Spain, its people, and its Church, as are some university offerings (at least according to Dr. Powell)?

So what do Chicano Studies departments promote? There appears to be no general agreement. One professor informed me that Chicano culture started when Cortés landed in Mexico in 1519. A couple of Chicano professors in southern California have told me their emphasis is on *indigenous* people, not Hispanos.

A text used in some Chicano courses, *Occupied America: A History of Chicanos* by Rodolfo Acuña, states the Pueblo Revolt was caused by Spanish abuses and that *"Eventually the rebels were tried in Spanish courts, and received severe punishments in the form of hanging, whipping, dismemberment (of hands or feet) or condemnation to slavery."* This confusion of the Acoma War of 1599 and the Pueblo Revolt of 1680 is actually used as a basic text in some Chicano Studies departments.

Do Chicano courses address realities in the USA? A student in a Chicano course informed me no one had ever brought up historical items like the Dred Scott Decision.

History is the most dangerous field of study in American society. It is no simple task to discover what writer is genuine and who has an axe to grind. Was Oñate a hero? Was Po'pay? Who is telling the historical truth about the Pueblo Revolt? Was it actually the St. Lawrence Day Massacre? Should

106

we believe Silverberg, Knaut, Archuleta, etc.? Or should we believe Bolton, Hanke, Simmons, etc.? Does Po'pay actually represent all New Mexicans in Statuary Hall? The reader must decide.

While the statue can be said generally to laud the Pueblo people, which is well and good, one can only wonder if the Pueblos are aware of basic Amerindian historical realities in what is now the USA. For example, groups of Lower Creeks, Cherokees, and Choctaw warriors helped Andrew Jackson defeat the Red Sticks at the 1814 Battle of Horseshoe Bend. A few months later he took some 8,000,000 acres of their lands for the USA. When he became President, Jackson saw to it that they were deported to Oklahoma, right along with the tribes they had helped conquer. In the West after the Apache Scouts were instrumental in capturing (1886) "renegades" like Geronimo, the Scouts were disarmed and put on the same train headed to dungeons in Florida. The study of history is indeed sobering, especially if you are a member of a targeted group.

There are many people who believe the study of History is a waste of time. *Who cares what happened hundreds of years ago?* They don't understand that studying History is the only secure way to recognizing one's reality, whether it be in Santa Fe or any other town in the State or the Southwest.

Marc Simmons has stated that a person who doesn't know history is *intellectually defenseless.* And being defenseless hurts targeted groups more than anybody else. It has also been observed that "modern" Hispanic New Mexicans are no more aware of their history than individuals who are fairly new arrivals to the State.

While New Mexico is steeped in history, New Mexicans have been required to learn about it for graduation from high school only since 2005. In many schools the required course begins with statehood in 1912, not 1598 with the settlement of the Knights of St. John. Does this tell impressionable students that *real history* started with statehood? Should we forget Spanish colonial history and the quarter century of Mexico? *Is that the reality Hispanics have to face if they are to be "good Americans"?*

Recognizing reality has everything to do with one's attitude, behavior, lifestyle, and living conditions. If students in elementary school are taught, *"Oñate hacked off the feet of the Acomas..."* most young people will grow up with the impression that *"Spaniards were cruel!"* It follows that the atrocities of the Pueblo Revolt will be interpreted as *"The first American Revolution!"* with Spaniards getting what they deserved for their cruel tyrannies. With such *horrible ancestors,* does it follow that Hispanic New Mexican people old and young should be approached with caution? Besides, *some people are quick to believe,* are they not part of the criminal element, part of the illegal drug scene, petty thieves, graffiti uglies, troublemakers, school dropouts, academic underachievers put in remedial classes? At the very least, it's better to ignore them, some people have come to believe. How prevalent are these attitudes in Santa Fe? Dr. Simmons is certainly correct: people who don't know their history are intellectually defenseless and the Hispanos of Santa Fe and New Mexico are paying the price for their lack of knowledge in accurate history concerning events like the Pueblo Revolt.

Propaganda as history has to be recognized before progress can be made in discovering the glories of New Mexican achievements like not exterminating or deporting the Pueblo people, like having the will to create the Comanche Peace with warlike tribes of the Great Plains, like Hispanos being ranked among the best horsemen in the world, like having the best civil rights record in the entire USA. So who is writing this kind of valid history? Perhaps Charles Fletcher Lummis, writing around 1891, summed it up best in his *A New Mexico David and Other Stories*:

> *I hope some day to see a real history of the United States; a history not written in a closet, from one-sided affairs, but based on a knowledge of the breadth of our history, and a disposition to do it justice, a book which will realize that the early history of this wonderful country is not limited to a narrow strip on the Atlantic seaboard, but that it began in the great Southwest...*
>
> *Before the oldest of the Pilgrim Fathers had been born, swarthy Spanish heroes were colonizing much of what is now the United States... in their little corner of which they suffered for 350 years such awful dangers and hardships as our Saxon forefathers did not dream of. I hope to see such a history, which will do justice to perhaps the most wonderful pioneers the world has ever produced...*
>
> *When that history is written you will find thrilling matter in the story of New Mexico..."*